This book is to be returned on or before the date above.
It may be borrowed for a further period if not in demand.

LIBRARIES

1 Broad St Hemel Hempstead Herts HP2 5BW
Tel; 0442 63461 Fax; 0442 217102

Copyright; Jim Sperinck 1994

To obtain information about acting fees payable on all professional and amateur performances of this play, together with any other details, please apply to the publishers;

Jasper Publishing

1 Broad Street Hemel Hempstead
Herts HP2 5BW
Tel; 0442 63461 Fax; 0442 217102

A licence must first be obtained before any performance can be given, and fees are payable in advance.

ISBN 1 874009 75 9

CHARACTERS

Sultan Shahriar	Ruler of Baghdad
Sultana Schererazade	His wife
Princess Raisin	Their daughter
Ahmed, The Kalandar Prince	Suitor to Raisin
Mesrour	The Sultan's Executioner
Sinbad	A sailor
Kashoo	Sinbad's girlfriend
Widow Duffcake	Sinbad's mother & Palace Cook
Omar Khayyam	Widow Duffcake's other son
Marco Polo	Friend of Omar Khayyam
Kaliban - El Krookid	Kaliph of Kufabad
Ali Baba	Henchman to Kaliban
Genius, Slave of the Lamp	Slave to Kaliban
Eric	Ghostly Echo of the cave
Dragon	

Chorus as; townspeople, palace guards and servants, maidens, slave girls and dancers, bazaar stallholders and shoppers, courtiers, mini-dragons etc.,

SYNOPSIS OF SCENES

ACT 1

ACT 2

Scenery may be kept very simple if desired. Alternatively, this pantomime offers the opportunity to put on a really lavish production - the choice is yours. There is a short, interact scene between each of the main scenes that will allow sufficient time for scene changes. These interact scenes can easily be played in front of tabs, or, if facilities allow, with a frontcloth flown.

Most principals can wear the same costume throughout the show, with the possible exception of the finale scene. Please refer to the Production Notes at the end of the script.

NOTES ON THE CHARACTERS

Sultan Shahriar. A pompous, overbearing, but otherwise quite jovial type, that the audience will want to laugh at. A small part, but with two important songs to sing. Male.

Schererazade. A stately, patient companion to Shahriar, in keeping with the story-telling original character. Female.

Princess Raisin. The more "queenly" of the two principal girls, and with a smaller part. She is at ease with her father, and is the only one who dares to tell him off. Female.

Ahmed, The Kalandar Prince. A rich, visiting suitor to Raisin. A formal lover, again in keeping with the original character. The more stately of the two principal boys. Female.

Mesrour. The Sultan's Executioner, with a wicked sense of humour. A minor part. Male.

Sinbad. The premier principal boy. A more "working class" type, than Ahmed. Female.

Kashoo. Constant companion and girlfriend of Sinbad. Again, the less stately of the two principal girls. Female.

Widow Duffcake. The typical Pantomime Dame. Saucy, emotional, mad-cap, feather-brained, outrageously dressed, volatile and energetic. Male.

Omar Khayyam. Widow Duffcake's other son. A dreamer and poet. Half of a comedy pair with Marco Polo. Female or male.

Marco Polo. An explorer. The other half of the comedy pair. Female or male.

Kaliban. The heavy baddie. To be booed at all times. Intent on stealing the magic Kalandar Stone, a wedding-gift from Ahmed, and which, if stolen, will bring catastrophe to the city of Baghdad. Male.

Ali Baba. Rogue and henchman to Kaliban. Male.

Genius, Slave of the Lamp. Aladdin's Genie in a former existence. Now Kaliban's slave. A key role. The third, but reluctant, part of the evil trio, who finds a way to transfer the balance of power over to the "good" side, without disobeying his master. Male, but could be female.

Eric, the Ghostly Echo. An unexpected discovery in the Dragon's Cave. Male or female.

Dragon. Kaliban's guardian of the Magic Stone. He turns out to have a bark worse than his bite. Can be played by one, large male, or by two (panto horse style) or by a team of juniors (Chinese Festival Dragon style).

Mini-dragons. Junior, cuddly versions of the Dragon. Male or female.

AUTHOR'S NOTE

This is the seventh in this series of traditional pantomimes. All of the pantomimes in the series incorporate the fundamental, and essential ingredients of; easily recognised characters, and a story line that is strong, and around which all the music and humour is woven.

They are all primarily written, of course, for a younger audience, but hopefully with something for everyone who loves a good traditional pantomime.

The scripts are specially written for amateur production, drawing on my twenty years or so of involvement in this area, at all levels. There is nothing included here that will be difficult to stage. by either school, or amateur groups.

Although "**An Arabian Nights Panto**" may be a less familiar title in the world of pantomime, it will hopefully appeal to those looking for something a little different to present to their audiences. Many of the Arabian Nights stories are established favourites with everyone anyway; The Young Prince and The Young Princess, The Voyages of Sinbad, Ali Baba and the Forty Thieves etc., with such well-known characters as; Sultan Shahriar, Schererazade, The Kalandar Prince and many others. It offers one more welcome opportunity to present a lavish, "oriental type" production, that is always so popular. It also offers your audience a chance to see many favourites, all together in one pantomime; Sinbad, Ali Baba, A Genie in a Lamp etc., as well as the traditional Dame, Baddie and henchmen, and comedy pair. For a thriving group there is the additional opportunity to show off two pairs of principals boys and principal girls.

I wish you every success with this pantomime.

Jim Sperinck

MUSICAL NUMBERS

The songs and music included here are suggestions only for the type of material that can be used. Final choice is left to the Musical Director.

Please note that permission from **Jasper Publishing** to perform this play does not include permission to use copyright songs and music. Performers are urged to consult the **Performing Right Society** (see note below).

If you experience any difficulty in obtaining music for this show, we recommend that you try: **Tim Evans, Tempo, PO Box 173, Pinner, Middlesex HA5 3PP**

Overture - Music from the Symphonic Suite "Schererazade" by Rimsky-Korsakov, or other theme music

Act 1

1.	Opening chorus, "On a Wonderful Day Like Today" or "Not Since Nineveh" or another	Full chorus number
2.	"Major-General Stanley's Song" from The Pirates of Penzance, or another	Solo from Sultan, with chorus backing
3.	"Diamonds are a Girl's Best Friend" or "I'm just an Old-Fashioned Girl" or another	Solo from Widow Duffcake
4.	"Stranger in Paradise" or "Shall we Dance" or "Who's been Polishing the Sun?" or another	Duet; Raisin & Ahmed
5.	Optional, "Lovejoy" or "Antiques Roadshow" music	
6.	Music from "Schererazade" or another	Dance of the Harem slaves
7.	"The Sheikh of Araby" or "I'm the Tops" or another	Omar, Sultan and chorus

8.   "Who Will Buy" or "Baubles, Bangles   Full chorus
     and Beads" or "The Old Bazaar in
     Baghdad (Cairo)" or another

9.   "You've Got to Pick a Pocket" or "We're   Trio; Kaliban, Ali Baba
     in the Money" or "Money Makes the   and Genius
     World go Around"

10. "Wish Me Luck as you Wave me   Widow Duffcake, Omar,
     Goodbye" or "High Hopes" or another   Sinbad, Kashoo and
                                                    Marco

Act 2

11. "Firebird Suite" or "In the Hall of the   Junior chorus dance
     Mountain King" or "March of the
     Siamese Children"

12. "When You've Got Friends" or "Consider   Chorus
     Yourself at Home" or "Fortuosity"

13. "Kiss me Honey, Honey, Kiss me" or   Kaliban and Widow
     "Anything You Can Do, I Can Do Better"   Duffcake
     or "Don't Throw Bouquets at Me" or
     "Big Spender"

14. "Raindrops Keep Falling on (his) Head"   Chorus
     or "Born Free" or "It's a Hap, Hap,
     Happy Day"

15. "Sheikh of Araby" reprise, or another   Community number

16. "On a Wonderful Day Like Today" or   Finale, full chorus
     any up-tempo number from the show

*The following statement (provided by the **Performing Right Society Ltd.,**) concerning the use of music, is included here for your attention.*

The permission of the owner of the performing right in copyright music must be obtained before any public performance may be given, whether in conjunction with a play or sketch or otherwise, and this permission is just as necessary for amateur performances as for professional. The majority of copyright musical works (other than oratorios, musical plays and similar dramatico-musical works) are controlled in the British Commonwealth by the **Performing Right Society Ltd., 29-33 Berners Street, London W1P 4AA.**

The Society's practice is to issue licences authorising the use of its repertoire to the proprietors of premises at which music is publicly performed, or, alternatively, to the organisers of musical entertainment, but the Society does not require payment of fees by performers as such. Producers or promoters of plays, sketches etc., at which music is to be performed, during or after the play or sketch, should ascertain whether the premises at which the performances are to be given are covered by a licence issued by the Society, and if they are not, should make application to the Society for particulars as to the fee payable.

Also available in this series

Aladdin
Babes in the Wood
The Canterbury Tales Panto
Dick Whittington
Red Riding Hood
Robinson Crusoe

AN
ARABIAN NIGHTS
PANTO

ACT 1

Overture

After the overture, to a dramatic chord, the curtains open, and the opening number begins

Scene 1

The scene is a market place, outside the palace in old Baghdad. the crowd are awaiting the arrival of the Kalandar Prince who is to marry Princess Raisin, the daughter of Sultan Shahriar, ruler of Baghdad, and his wife the Sultana Schererazade. It is a colourful scene with the stage filled with bustling spectators; citizens, market traders, street urchins, pickpockets, palace soldiers etc., all hoping to catch a glimpse of the Prince as he passes by

Song No 1

Opening full-chorus number, sung by all on stage, "On a Wonderful Day Like Today" or "Not Since Nineveh" or another

At the end of the song the chorus mingle and chatter

Enter Marco Polo and Omar Khayyam

Omar Oh look Marco, there's people out there. What do they want?
Marco That's an audience Omar.
Omar What, like with the queen?
Marco What?
Omar An audience with the queen.
Marco THE QUEEN! She's not out there, is she?

They both peer into the audience

Omar I can't see any tiaras or anything.
Marco No. Not even a corgi.
Omar Better stand to attention, just in case.

They both stand to attention

Marco I bet she can't stand still like this.
Omar Who, the queen?
Marco No, Anneka Rice.
Omar She's not here as well is she?
Marco Probably on a royal visit.
Omar Who, Anneka Rice?
Marco No, the queen.
Omar She's a keep-fit fanatic you know.
Marco Who, the queen?
Omar and **Marco** *(together)* No. Anneka Rice.
Marco *(jogging on the spot)* I do a lot of keep-fit.
Omar Do you?
Marco Yes. I want a body to match my mind.
Omar Then you'd be invisible.
Marco I go to keep-fit classes every Wednesday.
Omar Yes. With a sick-note from your mum.
Marco And I run ten miles every day.
Omar Yes. The trouble is, by Sunday you're seventy miles from home.

They both relax, tired of standing to attention and jogging

Marco Whew! That's enough of that.
Omar *(indicating the audience)* Shall we ask them to help us?
Marco Good idea. *(to audience)* We've got a really important job for you to do. Would you like to help us?
Audience Yes.
Omar They don't sound very sure do they? Ask them again.
Marco *(to audience)* I'm only going to let you help if you shout out really loud this time. Will you help us?
Audience Yes.
Marco Good. Now this is what we want you to do. There's a really horrible man coming on in a minute, and we want you to give him a big boo. Right?
Audience Yes.
Omar A really loud, yelling, noisy, horrible, enormous boo. Can you do that?
Audience Yes.
Marco And we want you to boo him every time you see him. OK?
Audience Yes.
Omar Good. Get ready. Here he comes now.

Green spot on wings, and crash on cymbals as, enter Kaliban with lamp round neck. Omar and Marco get audience to boo

Kaliban Out of my way! I want to see the Kalandar Prince arrive. *(to audience)* And don't boo me when I come on! Who told you to do that? *(pointing to Omar and Marco)* Was it them?

Omar and Marco whistle and look very innocent as the audience responds

Marco It wasn't us.
Omar No.
Kaliban Now, I'm going to go off...
Marco He's been going off for years.
Omar *(holding his nose)* Whew! Yes.
Kaliban Do you mind! When I come on again, I want you to cheer this time.

Kaliban exits. Omar and Marco encourage the audience to boo even louder.

Enter Kaliban, to crash on cymbals and boos from the audience

Kaliban That's not a cheer! Don't you know how to cheer? You go 'Hooray',
   like that. It's these two, isn't it? Clear off you.

Omar and Marco exit, laughing

Chorus 1 *(pointing off stage)* Look! The Kalandar Prince arrives!
Chorus 2 There he is!

A general buzz of, "Here he is" "Over there" "The Prince arrives" "Look" etc.,

*Enter, to a fanfare, The Kalandar Prince and his attendants, one of whom is
carrying a large jewel on a silk cushion*

The buzz of excitement turns to a cheer

*From the palace side enter: Sultan Shahriar, Schererazade, Raisin and their
entourage, including Mesrour the Executioner. They meet The Kalandar Prince
centre stage*

Sultan Greetings Kalandar Prince. You have been on a long journey.
Prince Yes Sultan. And my feet are singing.
Sultan Well let's hope they make a better sound than this lot here.

*General chorus of, "What a cheek!" "Who does he think he is?" "I suppose he
thinks that's funny?" etc., At a hand signal from the Sultan the crowd fall
immediately silent, as though suddenly turned off*

Sultan *(indicating his wife)* My wife the Sultana Schererazade and I look
   forward to your marriage to our daughter.
Schererazade Greetings Kalandar Prince.
Prince Greetings.
Schererazade May I introduce to you our uncle the Kaliban El Krookid,
   Kaliph of Kufabad.

Kaliban steps forward and kisses Prince on both cheeks

Kaliban Greetings Kalandar Prince.
Prince Greetings sire.
Sultan *(to Kaliban)* Right now give him his wallet back.

Kaliban pulls a face and hands over a wallet to Prince

(to Prince) You've got to watch yourself when he's around. *(pointing to Raisin)* And this is my daughter Raisin. You'll be seeing more of her later.
Raisin Don't be rude father!
Sultan *(all innocence)* What did I say?
Raisin Greetings Kalandar Prince.
Prince Greetings Raisin. *(beckoning the servant with the stone forward)* As a wedding gift I bring a jewel of great renown, the Kalandar stone.

Servant with stone comes forward and kneels. The crowd gasp in wonderment

Sultan A wondrous stone indeed.
Kaliban *(greedily)* Yes, it must be worth a fortune. *(aside to audience)* It's wasted on them.
Prince It has magical powers, great Sultan. But it's beauty dims before that of your daughter.
Schererazade I wonder which charm school he went to?
Raisin Why thank you Prince.

More gasps from the crowd

Sultan Magical powers? You haven't nicked it from Paul Daniels, have you?
Prince Whoever possesses the stone will rule this kingdom, but, if the stone is stolen, the people will fall into a deep slumber.
Sultan Well, they're half asleep anyway!

The crowd protest amongst themselves "Do you mind?" "Cheek!" "Really thinks he's somebody!" *etc., The Sultan does the hand-signal again and the crowd fall immediately silent*

Kaliban A deep slumber you say?
Prince Until the Kalandar stone is returned to its rightful owner, yes.
Kaliban *(to audience)* That's going to be unfortunate for them when I've got it.
Sultan Huh! Most of them laze about doing nothing all day anyway, it'll be hard to tell the difference.

Outraged responses from the crowd again, "Well really!" "This is too much" "How dare he?" *etc., Sultan does his hand signal again and the crowd fall immediately silent*

Silence! No insultan the Sultan! *(to the Prince)* Watch this. *(to the crowd)* Down!

All grumble, then kneel or bow low

Up!

All stand up

He, he! Good, isn't it? Down!

All moan again and kneel or bow low

Up!

All stand up again

(to the Prince) There you see? It's like playing mass yo-yos! It's wonderful to have power! Here, you have a go.
Prince Thank you sire. *(to the crowd)* Er, down.

The crowd stand and look at each other

Chorus 1 Huh! I should think so!
Chorus 2 Power mad, the lot of them!
Chorus 3 Not a chance mate!
Prince They're taking no notice of me.
Sultan Strange! Your name's not John Major is it? Never mind. I'll teach you when I have a moment to spare from the arduous pressures of civic duties. All those expense account lunches and things. Now where were we?
Kaliban Er, the beautiful, valuable Kalandar stone sire. *(craftily)* Shall I look after it for you?
Sultan No thanks. I'm still waiting for my lawn-mower back. The one you borrowed last year.
Schererazade Putting you in charge of the stone, would be like hiring a crocodile for a swimming instructor.
Raisin Thank you very much Prince. It is a most generous gift.
Prince Only the best will ever be good enough for you Princess Raisin.

"A's" from the crowd

Sultan *(calls)* Where's my Executioner? Mesrour!
Prince *(alarmed)* What did I say?

Mesrour, standing beside the Sultan, steps forward, almost knocking him over

Mesrour Sire?
Sultan Watch it you fool! You nearly drew blood there! Guard this stone with your life, or something even more important. If anyone comes near it *(runs finger across throat)* I won't bother you with the details, but carry out the usual itinerary. You know, bits nailed to the city gates, bits boiled in oil, that sort of thing...

Mesrour It will be a pleasure sire.
Sultan Their legs will turn to jelly, when they are taken into custody.
Mesrour Jelly and custardy. Oh very good sire, if I may say so...
Sultan No you may not. One more joke like that and it's tea towels for you.
Mesrour *(bowing low)* I think you mean "curtains" master.
Sultan Whoever heard of an executioner with a sense of humour? Now, pay
attention.

Song No 2

Solo from the Sultan, backed by those on stage. "I'm the Tops" or, to the tune of
"Major-General Stanley's Song", the following words are suggested

Sultan I am the Sultan Shahriar, I'd like to sing an aria.
It won't take long, so settle back, not more than half-an-hour-ier.
I have a mass of untold wealth, and shares in British Telecom.
A mattress filled with ten pound notes for me to go to bed upon.
I've wardrobes full of latest modes, and shirts styled by Yves Saint
Laurent.
I've property both here and there, from Nineveh to Babylon,
And dungeons that I hardly use, except when there's a riot on.
And every comfort known to man, of that you can depend upon.

All repeat three times
And every comfort known to man, of that you can depend upon.

Sultan From every country known to man, as far as far Manchuria,
Come gifts from many wealthy fans, delivered by fast courier.
I'm rather like that Genghis Khan, but just a trifle cru-ell-er.
In short, the very model of a fine despotic ru-el-er.

All He's rather like that Genghis Khan, but just a trifle cru-ell-er.
In short, the very model of a fine despotic ru-el-er.

Sultan I am the very model of a fine despotic ru-el-er.
Now despotism's in decline, we're few-er-er and few-er-er.
Gold ornamental trappings, in rare patterns most peculiar,
Are fashioned by my oriental, overpaid court jeweller.
I'm very well acquainted with all matters diabolical.
And punishments for sundry crimes, I've listed categorical.
My every whim is instant law, and must be satisfied therefore,
As very well befits a very fine despotic ru-el-er.

all repeat three times
As very well befits a very fine despotic ru-el-er.

Sultan An unpaid bill, a small complaint, will instantly secure,
An introduction to my overworked top executioner.

My every whim is instant law, and must be satisfied therefore.
I am the very model of a fine despotic ru-el-er.

All   His every whim is instant law, and must be satisfied therefore.
He is the very model of a fine despotic ru-el-er.

At the end of the song

Sultan Now let us to the palace. *(as they exit)* You must be hungry. It's corn beef hash tonight, and plum pudding. I love Fridays, it's my favourite.

Sultan and entourage exit with Prince and his servants. Some of the chorus exit also. Kaliban remains

Kaliban The magic Kalandar stone eh? *(pointing to himself)* Soon it will be my stone. I'm going to nick it. Oh yes I am.
Audience Oh no you're not.
Kaliban Yes I am.
Audience No you're not.
Kaliban Yes, yes, yes yes, I am. So there. Don't argue, it's rude. *(holding up the lamp, as the audience shout at him)* I bet you don't know what this is?
Audience It's a magic lamp. *(etc.,)*
Kaliban No it's not. It's a magic lamp. I bet you don't know what's inside.
Audience A Genie.
Kaliban A Genie? You think you know everything, don't you?
Audience Yes.
Kaliban Alright clever clogs, how do you get the Genie out then? I bet you don't know that.
Audience Rub the lamp!
Kaliban Rub the lamp? Here, you've been here before, haven't you? You're not spies, are you? Because you know what I do to spies? I mince 'em up. Yes, I love minced spies, specially at Christmas.

The audience will be shouting at him

So you rub the lamp eh? What, like this? *(he pretends to be about to rub the lamp)*
Audience Yes.
Kaliban You sure? Like this? *(again pretending to be about to rub the lamp)*
Audience Yes.
Kaliban You think I'm going to, don't you?
Audience Yes!
Kaliban Well I'm not. So there. Ha, ha! Fooled you. I'm going to find my friend Ali Baba. He'll help me steal the magic stone. And don't boo me when I go off.

Kaliban exits, the audience boos. Kaliban returns

I told you not to boo me when I go off.

Kaliban exits again. The audience boos again

Enter Widow Duffcake and Sinbad from the other side

Widow Duffcake Here! They're not booing us, are they Sinbad?
Sinbad I hope not. *(to audience)* You're not booing us, are you?
Audience No.
Widow Duffcake Good. Because I'll soon get down there and sort you lot out. Now, stand here Sinbad we're bound to see him on his way to the palace. Not much of a crowd is it? I suppose *(local team)* are playing at home.

Some of the crowd take an interest in her

Chorus 1 Who are you looking for?
Widow Duffcake Oh aren't kids nosy? We're going to watch the Kalandar Prince go by. He's going to marry Princess Raisin.

The chorus laugh

And what's funny about that?
Chorus 2 You've missed him you nitwit!
Widow Duffcake Missed him? I haven't even thrown anything at him yet!
Chorus 3 He's gone by already.
Widow Duffcake *(to the audience)* He hasn't, has he?
Audience Yes.
Widow Duffcake What was that? *(to Sinbad)* I didn't hear anything did you? *(to audience)* Louder this time. Has he gone?
Audience YES!
Widow Duffcake No he hasn't!
Audience Yes he has!
Widow Duffcake Oh no he hasn't!
Audience Oh yes he has!
Widow Duffcake Well why didn't you say so! Wasting my time! I've got better things to do than stand here and watch nobody go by.
Sinbad Mother I told you not to spend so much time doing your hair.
Widow Duffcake Doing my hair? I'll do you in a minute! I've got to look beautiful haven't I? I might be seen by royalty.
Sinbad I hope not mother. There's probably a law against looking like that!
Widow Duffcake Such a sweet boy - he doesn't mean it! *(kicks him)*
Sinbad Ouch!
Widow Duffcake I'll have you know I've got magnetism.
Sinbad *(to the audience)* She means rheumatism.
Widow Duffcake Oh yes, I can see it now - Suddenly, across a crowded room, my prince looks at me, our eyes meet, and he lets out a weak cry...
Sinbad Help!
Widow Duffcake I remind him of something...

Sinbad Something in Jurassic Park.
Widow Duffcake He goes down on one knee...
Sinbad He's fainting with shock...
Widow Duffcake He wants to meet me.
Sinbad At the plastic surgeon's.
Widow Duffcake And bingo - I'm sitting on a marshmallow eating a silk cushion - or something like that - instead of slaving over a hot refrigerator all day. I hope he finds me soon, while I've still got the bloom of youth on my cheeks, and the cheeks of youth in my...
Sinbad Mother!
Chorus 3 You've certainly waited long enough!
Chorus 2 A couple of centuries too long!
Chorus 1 Put you in the royal zoo, more like!
Widow Duffcake How dare you! Clear off!

The crowd disperse. The junior chorus laughing at her as they go

Sinbad Mother we'd better be going. You've got to cook the Sultan's supper.
Widow Duffcake Oh go and tell them to start without me Sinbad.
Sinbad What shall I tell them to cook?
Widow Duffcake Tagliatelle.
Sinbad I thought he played for Inter-Milan.
Widow Duffcake That's Tortelini, you fool.
Sinbad Oh.
Widow Duffcake And tell them to nip down to *(local shop)* and get a couple of tins of Whiskas.
Sinbad Whiskas! You can't give the Sultan that!
Widow Duffcake What? No! I forgot to feed the royal cats this morning, silly.
Sinbad Oh right. *(exits)*

During the next speech Widow Duffcake may go down into the audience and ad lib if desired. If she does, the house lights should come up, and go down again when she returns to the stage

Widow Duffcake Oh I don't know what I'm doing here. Really I don't. I'm not from round here you know. No. You knew that didn't you? Yes, you could tell. I can tell you could tell. Yes, I'm from *(local area)* you see. You're dying to know how I ended up in the desert here, aren't you? What? Well I'm going to tell you anyway, so settle back for a few hours. You see I read all about how those naughty sultans keep women in those harems and things, and they just laze about all day dressed in beautiful silks, bathing in expensive perfumes, and eating Turkish delight. Shocking, isn't it? So I thought, that's not right is it? Why can't I get some of that! Well it's got to beat being on Social Security in *(local town)* hasn't it? So I smuggled away on the first boat leaving for neurotic places. I booked for Casablanca, well, I've always wanted to meet Humphrey Bogart you see! But I ended up here. But would they let me in? No! A beautiful creature like me! You can't believe it, can you? Nasty guards with long scimitar things kept prodding me. Really! *(rubbing her backside)* They're sharp those things. I've got the appointment with out-patients to prove it! Then this Sultan, you know, that one just now, Old Crinkley-Bottom, he came up to me and said, 'How many things can you do with asparagus tips?' Cheeky devil! I told him he'd have to marry me to find that out! Then he said, 'I've got just the job for you my little oil painting.' Yes, that's what he called me! Well, 'you old master' he said actually - but it's the same thing, isn't it? So I thought, hello, here we go - night work again! So here I am - chief cook at the palace. Well I've got to do something to support my poor boys - there's Sin-bad, and there's his brother - sins even worse! He he! No, just my little joke - Omar his name is - Omar Khayyam - He's no use at all! All he does is write silly poetry all day.

Enter Omar, with hand-held recording machine, and Marco hiding a rubber hammer behind his back

Omar *(speaking dramatically into the machine)* Awake for morning in the bowl of night...
Widow Duffcake Don't carry on, you'll give us all a fright! He he!
Omar Oh mother! You've ruined my flow now!
Widow Duffcake Flow! I'll ruin your flow alright. Where do you pick up all this common plumber's language?
Marco Widow Duffcake, talking of flows, what's a cure for water on the knee?
Widow Duffcake Oh, that's easy. A cure for water on the knee - drain-pipe trousers.
Marco And what's a cure for water on the brain?
Widow Duffcake Er. I don't know.
Marco *(craftily producing the hammer)* A tap on the head!

Marco taps her on the head, laughing and smiling at the audience. Widow Duffcake goes to the wings and receives a giant (blow-up) hammer and brings it on. Marco gets nervous, as Widow Duffcake relishes the moment

Widow Duffcake And here's one I prepared earlier.

Marco makes to exit

Where are you going?
Marco I've forgotten something.
Widow Duffcake What?
Marco I don't know - I've forgotten - I just told you.
Widow Duffcake Come here you horrible boy.

Marco obeys, slowly. When he is half-way to her he stops. Widow Duffcake measures the distant with the hammer and decides she cannot reach

Closer.

Marco edges a little closer. Widow Duffcake measures again

Closer.

Marco edges closer again, pulling a face. To a crash, Widow Duffcake boffs him over the head and he runs round the stage howling

(to the audience) Take no notice, he's a few steroids short of a gold medal.
Omar Mother I intend to be a famous poet one day.
Widow Duffcake Poets aren't famous 'til they've been dead for a few hundred years, you nitwit. There's no money in that. You're about as useful as a Citizens Charter! Sinbad's got his boat, and catches fish. And even Marco Polo here goes off exploring and selling spices and things...

All move forward, Widow Duffcake between Marco and Omar, as the curtains close behind them. The rest of the scene is played in front of tabs to allow the harem scene to be set up

Marco Yes, I'm a new-age traveller.
Widow Duffcake Yes and...
Marco I've got this beautiful camel you see.
Widow Duffcake So I...
Marco His name's Cuthbert, Cuthbert the camel, and...
Widow Duffcake And I...
Marco We've travelled all over - Egypt, Japan...
Widow Duffcake Here! Do you mind! I was here first!
Marco And China, and Morocco and...
Widow Duffcake Gawd! Will you stop talking when I'm interrupting? Duffcake will duff you up in a minute.

She is about to hit Marco again with the hammer, when Omar starts

Omar *(dramatically into the machine)* A book of verse beneath the bough. A jug of wine, a loaf of bread, and thou...
Widow Duffcake If you two don't pack it in right now. I'll chuck the pair of you in the canal!
Omar That's no way to talk to a sensitive genius.
Widow Duffcake No, but it's a good way to talk to you.
Omar You're ruining my couplets!
Widow Duffcake Oh I wish I could think of an answer to that!
Marco And I've discovered a new sweet.
Widow Duffcake Who wound you up again? You've discovered a new sweet Marco Polo?
Marco Yes. It's all round and minty, with a hole in the middle. I'm thinking of naming it after me.
Widow Duffcake Really Marco Polo? You're going to name these mints with the hole in the middle after yourself?
Marco Yes.
Widow Duffcake I wonder what you are going to call them? *(to audience)* Wait for it.

Dramatic chord

Marco Marco Mints.
Widow Duffcake Marco Mints! What a stupid name! It'll never catch on.
Omar Life's but a checker-board of nights and days...
Widow Duffcake I can't get a word in here sideways! I know! *(slyly to audience)* I think I'll sing a song.
Marco Oh dear!
Omar Ah! Mother - we must be off!

Widow Duffcake hands one of them the hammer. Omar and Marco exit quickly, putting their fingers in their ears as they go

Widow Duffcake Yes, you must be off. I thought I could smell something! *(shouting after them)* Wash your feet! And take your shoes and socks off first! That got rid of them! Oh I wish I could get my hands on that Kalandar Stone that I've heard about. I could wear it round my neck for good luck. Come to think of it, with that round my neck, who'd need good luck?

Song No 3

This is a solo from Widow Duffcake. "Diamonds are a Girl's Best Friend", or "I'm Just an Old Fashioned Girl" or another

At the end of the song Widow Duffcake exits

Scene 2

The palace harem. Luxuriant cushions are towards the back of the stage on which the Sultan and Sultana will sit when the chorus are dancing

Enter The Kalandar Prince on one side, and Princess Raisin from the other

Prince Ah, Princess.
Raisin Kalandar Prince. I was on my way to find you.
Prince *(bowing)* Indeed. Then I am the most fortunate of men.
Raisin Look. You don't have to keep all that formal stuff up when we're alone.
Prince Formal stuff?
Raisin You know, "May your camels never get the hump" and everything.
Prince Oh. I am sorry that I do not please you Princess.
Raisin Oh, I wouldn't say that. Call me Raisin, will you? And what shall I call you? I cannot keep calling you the Kalandar Prince.
Prince My name is Ahmed.
Raisin Good. Well that's the first bit sorted Ahmed. Now, you must learn to relax man. Be less formal. Let the cool vibes flow over you.
Prince It is truly a strange language that you speak Princess.
Raisin You'll soon pick it up.

Prince I will try, if you will help me.
Raisin *(taking his hand)* Perhaps it's all in a song somewhere.

Song No 4

*A duet from Raisin and Kalandar Prince, "Stranger in Paradise", or "Who's been
Polishing the Sun" or "Shall we Dance" or another*

At the end of the song

Raisin Now Ahmed, let me show you around the town.
Prince That would be most gracious of you Princess.
Raisin *(checking him)* Ah!
Prince I mean, Let's go babe. Let's - hit the hut.
Raisin *(not convinced)* Hmm, I suppose that is an improvement.

They both exit

*Green spot up, and crash on the cymbals, as Kaliban enters with magic lamp
around neck*

Kaliban Don't boo when I come on.
Audience Boo.
Kaliban I said... er, what's the use? Did you see that soppy pair? They won't
be so happy in a minute. From now on it gets very ugly - starting with me.
And don't make your own jokes up. I am the great Kaliban El Krookid,
Kaliph of Kufabad? See if you can say that six times quickly! A right little
medieval Schwarzenneger I am. Like your Maths teacher - only worse.
(indicating the lamp) See this? It's my secret weapon! Ha, ha! You think I'm
going to rub it, don't you?
Audience Yes.
Kaliban Well I am, so there. *(rubs the lamp)*
              Man United *(or local team)* start at three.
              Score a hat-trick - home for tea!

There is a bang and a flash, and Genius steps out of the smoke

Genius What is your wish, oh master?
Kaliban Gawd! I wish you'd learn to arrive a bit quieter for a start!
Genius I use the time-honoured, traditional approach master. Well suited to
English pantomime season. *(to audience)* I am available for children's
parties, school celebrations and etceteras. I can perform wondrous feats of
magic...
Kaliban Do you mind! Leave your feet out of this. You're under contract to
me. Look, the Kalandar stone is around here somewhere. A fabulous thing of
great wealth and magical powers.
Genius A fabulous thing of great wealth and magical powers? Like Paul
Daniels you mean?

Kaliban Paul Daniels? How does he keep getting in here?

Genie *(closing his eyes and concentrating hard)* Ah yes, master I see it now. At this moment it is safely guarded by Mesrour, the Sultan's executioner.

Kaliban Well I want it, so how do I get my grubby little hands on it eh?

Genius Alas master, that will be very difficult.

Kaliban Difficult! Huh! Call yourself a magic Genie? Well, I have a plan you see. *(taking a fake stone from his pocket)* I'm going to take the real stone, and put this one in its place. No-one will know the difference.

Music No 5 (optional)

The "Antiques Roadshow" music may come up under the following, if desired

Genius May I see it master? Where did you obtain it?

Kaliban *(handing over the stone)* I found it when I was clearing out the attic.

Genius *(looking at it closely)* Most interesting. Early ninth century, Persian I think.

Kaliban It belonged to my grandmother.

Genius Really. It is quite rare. Pity it's got a chip just here.

Kaliban Yes, she used to throw it at us.

Genius Have you any idea of the value?

Kaliban No, she wasn't worth much. Bit of an old rat-bag really.

Genius I meant the stone.

Kaliban Oh. No.

Genius You should send it to my uncle, El Southerby, for valuation.

"Antiques Roadshow" music, if used, fades

Kaliban *(snatching the stone back)* Never mind all that Lovejoy. Take me to the real stone - so I can do a swop.

Genius You wish me to magically transport you master?

Kaliban Of course I do. Do you think, I'm going to get a cheap day return on the tube or something?

Genius It is half-price on the buses for old wrinklies like you.

Kaliban Watch it! Or you go back in the lamp for another hundred years.

Genius Humblest pardons master. I will do even better, I will summon the Kalandar stone to you.

Genius claps his hands. Kaliban and Genius move to the side of the stage

Enter Sultan and Schererazade with attendants and guards etc., Maidens take up positions on either side of the cushions with ostrich fans. Mesrour enters and stands rigidly to attention, keeping an eye on the Kalandar stone, which a slave brings in on a cushion

Genius *(pointing to the stone)* There, you see, it's over there. I think I'll go and lie down for a spell! Lie down for a spell! He, he! I kill myself. *(exits)*

Kaliban Yes. Somebody should.

Sultan *(to Mesrour)* What poor entertainment do you have for our Royal Person today?

Mesrour *(taking out a TV Times from his pocket)* There's not much on, on Thursdays.

Sultan Did you get that new Nintendo game?

Mesrour *(barely stifling a laugh)* I N-intended to, but I forgot!

Sultan Pathetic.

Mesrour You're not going to cut me into SEGA-ments, are you?

Sultan One more joke like that and it's pillow slips for you.

Mesrour I think you mean "curtains" master.

Sultan Now, entertainment. You're not going to send on that Tony Blackburn again I hope?

Mesrour No sire, we have confined him to the deepest dungeon.

Sultan The one with horrible snakes, and huge rats in it?

Mesrour No. The one with Terry Wogan in it sire.

Sultan Aha! Even better! He, he! We only need Des O'Connor, and we've got a full-house - bingo! Entertainment! I want entertainment!

The Sultan claps his hands. Sultan and Schererazade sit

Music No 6

The harem dancers enter and perform a dance to an appropriate tune, "The Schererazade Music" or another. There is an opportunity here also to use any speciality items that you have: jugglers, magicians, fire-eaters, acrobats etc.,

At the end of the performance the dancers exit

Sultan *(to Schererazade)* And now my dear, you were going to tell me that story about the three men, the Englishman, Irishman, and the Scotsman...

Schererazade It was the story of 'The Three Treasures of Ahmed' sire.

Sultan I knew it was three something. I haven't heard it before have I?

Schererazade No sire. The Prince Ahmed loved a young maiden of great beauty, but her father would not allow them to marry.

Sultan *(looking sad, and getting out a handkerchief)* It's not going to be one of those sad ones again, is it?

Schererazade It has a happy ending sire.

Sultan Yes but we never get to the end, do we?

Schererazade Now Prince Ahmed had two brothers, Hussein and Ali...

Kaliban steps forward, and Schererazade breaks off

Kaliban Sire.

Sultan *(annoyed)* I knew it! A short interruption in transmission again. It's like keep having power cuts in the middle of "Listen with Mother".

Schererazade We can finish it later sire.

Kaliban *(taking out the false stone and showing it to the audience)* I was most concerned to ensure that the wonderful stone, was being safely guarded sire.

Kaliban goes over to the stone as if to pick it up, but Mesrour bars his way and he finds himself at the nasty end of a scimitar

Kaliban You nearly drew blood there you fool!
Sultan As you can see Kaliban, it is safely guarded. In fact, if you get any closer, Mesrour will cut something off. Nothing important of course.
Kaliban What? Oh! Thank goodness for that!
Sultan Just your arms, your head, or whatever...
Kaliban *(looking down)* My whatever? I don't think I've got one of those.
Sultan Just be careful.
Kaliban Oh I will. *(slyly to the audience)* I'll be very careful, with plan B, next time. *(to the Sultan)* I wasn't going to touch it. *(to the audience)* No I wasn't. Shut up you.
Sultan *(as the audience respond to Kaliban)* The natives are restless tonight.
Kaliban *(with menace at the audience)* They'll be slumbering quietly soon.

Enter Widow Duffcake with large metal saucepan and ladle. She bangs the saucepan loudly, using it like a dinner gong. Everyone jumps at the noise

Widow Duffcake Not while I'm on! *(moving around the stage)* Dinner is served! Dinner is served...
Sultan Yes, alright...
Widow Duffcake Dinner is served! *(to audience)* Nobody sleeps while I'm around!
Sultan Gawd! Does she have to make all that noise?
Kaliban She should be reported to the Noise Abatement Society
Widow Duffcake Dinner is served! Come and get it!
Sultan I'll have to have her fitted with a silencer!

Enter the Kalandar Prince and Raisin

Raisin I've been showing Ahmed around the town father.
Schererazade You are just in time for dinner.
Prince I'm starving. What is it?
Widow Duffcake It's a nice sheep's-eye pudding.

Everyone groans and pulls faces

Sultan That should see us through the week.
Kaliban *(to audience)* The old jokes are best.
Widow Duffcake Do you mind not mocking my culinary expertise!
Sultan *(to Schererazade)* Didn't know she suffered from it.
Schererazade She doesn't - we do.
Kaliban Yes. I broke a tooth on her gravy last week.
Schererazade I know I'm not a good cook, but at least my gravy moves about.
Sultan Now before we eat, is there any more entertainment?

Widow Duffcake signals to the wings for Omar and Marco to come on. Enter Omar, very shy, pushed on by Marco

Widow Duffcake *(to Omar)* Come on, it's your big opportunity. Your very own Royal Command Performance.
Sultan Who is it, Hale and Pace?
Kaliban Looks more like Wilson, Kepple and Betty - without the Betty.
Widow Duffcake Don't be shy now. Tell them one of your nice poems.
Sultan *(to Mesrour)* Sharpen up your scimitar. In case he starts the one about the boy on the burning deck.
Mesrour It'll be blankets for him if he does.
Sultan You mean "curtains", you fool.
Widow Duffcake Come on Omar. Just pretend I'm not here.
All on stage We wish we didn't have to pretend.
Widow Duffcake OH!
Omar *(nervously bowing low)* Sire, if I may offer some humble entertainment. I have written a poem specially for the occasion.
Sultan *(to Kaliban)* I wrote a poem once - about an Eskimo called Nell.
Raisin Father, don't be rude.
Sultan *(all innocence)* What did I say?
Marco Get on with it Omar.
Omar *(summoning up his courage)* Very well.

Song No 7

Omar hesitantly starts his song, with encouragement from Widow Duffcake. Sultan sings the second verse, having picked up the idea. The last verse is sung by all, as they do a silly dance. To the tune of "The Sheikh of Araby"

Omar	You're the Sheikh of Araby...
Sultan	That's me.
Omar	All this belongs to thee.
Sultan	To me.
Omar	You're of the highest rank,
	You even own the bank.
	More camels than you can count,
	Are lined up out the front,
Sultan	And rented out by me,
	The Sheikh of Araby.

I'm the Sheikh of Araby.
So all bow down to me.
I'll let you pitch your tent,
For a quite modest rent.
My oasis holiday scheme,
Is working like a dream.
With profits all to me,
The Sheikh of Araby.

All on stage   He's the Sheikh of Araby.
As mean as he can be.
He'll have your rear end tanned,
If you nick a grain of sand.
The stars that shine at night,
He charges for the light.
We wish we could be free,
From the Sheikh of Araby.

All exit, led by the Sultan, doing the Hokey-Kokey. Last to go off is Widow Duffcake, banging the pan and yelling, "Dinner", as the curtains slowly close

Scene 3

A street on the way to the bazaar. This is played in front of tabs, or a frontcloth

Enter Genius

Genius That horrible Kaliban. He's going to make me steal the magic stone, and put everyone to sleep. Here he is. Give him a boo will you?

Enter Kaliban to boos

Kaliban Don't boo me. Now, I want you to steal the Kalandar stone.
Genius Master, if I steal the stone, a great misery will fall on the people.
Kaliban A great misery will fall on the people? What, like Patrick Moore or Bernard Manning, you mean? Ha! Remind me to buy shares in headache tablets! It's great isn't it? I love being horrible. *(indicating audience)* Don't worry about them. They don't look very happy anyway. No you don't.
Audience Oh yes we do.
Kaliban Not in a minute you won't.
Audience Oh yes we will.
Genius The people will fall into a deep sleep master.
Kaliban Well at least it'll shut them up. Ha, ha! Yes it will.
Audience No it won't.
Genius It would not be right master.
Kaliban Not be right! When did I ever worry about that? You're beginning to sound like that Jiminy Cricket.
Genius I never watch these strange English games.
Kaliban What?
Genius Cricket master.
Kaliban Jiminy Cricket you fool. From pino-knocky-what's-is-name. You'll be wanting to sing, "Always let your conscience be your guide" next.
Genius I will if you insist. But it's very confusing. I thought I was to be in Aladdin again this year. I've learnt my words and everything. Now I find I'm in this Arabian Nights thing, and you want me to sing a song from Pinocchio. I'll need a psychiatrist soon.

Kaliban Yes - you need a shrink - to get you back in the lamp! Ha, ha!
Genius I hate pantomimes.
Kaliban Stop moaning and get back to the script. What about this stone?
Genius I will need some assistance master.
Kaliban Let's get my old mate Ali Baba to help us. He works in the bazaar, so take us there.
Genius Can't we walk master? It's only round the corner.
Kaliban Walk? I don't want to walk! I want you to magic me there.
Genius It's a waste of good magic. Just because you're too lazy to walk.

Genius waves his arms, and to a crash the lights suddenly go out as the curtains open quickly. The lights come up and they are standing in the middle of the old bazaar

Scene 4

The old bazaar in Baghdad. The stage is filled with stalls selling; carpets, fabrics, spices, pots etc., Ali Baba's stall, with an array of pots, is on one side of the stage. One stall must have a carpet labelled "magic carpet". Shoppers are bustling about

Kaliban and Genius merge into the crowd

The merchants' cries ring out. Each trying to drown out the others

Merchant 1 Silks. Fine Eastern silks. Silks. Fine Eastern silks.
Merchant 2 Carpets. Buy my carpets. Carpets. Oriental and magic.
Merchant 3 Exotic spices today. Exotic spices today.
Ali Baba Pots. Beautiful pots. Pots. Beautiful pots.

The chants gradually merge into the chorus number, sung by all on stage

Song No 8

A full chorus number, "Who will Buy?" or "The Old Bazaar in Baghdad (Cairo)" or "Baubles, Bangles and Beads" or another

At the end of the song Kaliban greets Ali Baba. The rest of the chorus continue with their shopping, bartering with the merchants, chatting to each other and wandering on and off stage until they become frozen

Kaliban Ali Baba, my old friend. May your camels never go rusty.
Ali Baba Greetings oh mighty Kaliban. May your olive trees never get dry-rot. It is many moons since you visited my humble stall.
Kaliban How are things, oh renowned Ali Baba of the forty thieves?
Ali Baba Alas, times are hard sire. You see what I am reduced to. I might as well be working in *(local market)*. Since this infidel government got in I am dying the death of a thousand cut-backs.

Kaliban I told you not to vote for them. You wouldn't listen. Just because that politician promised not to put VAT on pottery...

Ali Baba If I could return to my troubles for a moment. I am now known as Ali Baba and the three and a half thieves. It is most humiliating.

Kaliban Three and a half thieves?

Ali Baba Yes, I've just taken on Ronny Corbett.

Kaliban Ah! My friend, your fortunes are about to change. If you help my servant here, you will be richly rewarded.

Ali Baba And who is this strange, untidy-looking servant with the diesel fume per-fume?

Genius Do you mind! You want to try living in an oil-lamp.

Ali Baba Ah! It gets on your WICK, does it?

Genius Not as much as you do.

Ali Baba Never mind. I'm sure it will be OIL right on the night!

Genius (to audience) Sometimes I hate pantomimes.

Ali Baba Don't get FLAMING mad! You'll just have to like it, or LAMP it!

Kaliban He'll turn you into something ugly and horrible.

Genius Too late - nature has beaten me to it.

Kaliban Look Ali Baba, this is the Genius of the lamp.

Ali Baba No, no. You mean the Genie of the lamp?

Genius Jeanie is a girl's name. Tell me, can you turn those pots into gold?

Ali Baba Alas no. Would that I could.

Genius I can. That is why I am called the Genius of the lamp.

Ali Baba (suddenly changing to a grovelling attitude) Ah. A thousand pardons sire. A man would be fortunate indeed to have you as his partner. Would you care to marry into the family perhaps? I have a young daughter, passing fair, of no more than fifteen summers...

Kaliban (checking him, and indicating higher) How many summers?

Ali Baba Well, perhaps, nineteen summers...

Seeing Kaliban still indicating higher

Would you believe twenty-five summers?

Kaliban Ali, you've been trying to get rid of that daughter of yours for twenty years to my knowledge.

Ali Baba (to audience) It's tough being a parent these days.

Kaliban We need your help Ali Baba. (confidentially in Ali's ear) We plan to steal the Kalandar stone, so that I can rule over the kingdom.

Ali Baba As ever my master's ambition is boundless! But it's dangerous. It is said the Executioner's eyes never close, and his scimitar is ever sharp.

Kaliban We must find a way Ali.

Genius An alley-way Ali.

Ali Baba (looking round to ensure he is not overheard, and whispering in Kaliban's ear) I know of a secret way into the palace - around the back - and through the cellar of my uncle Ali the hairdresser.

Kaliban (also secretive and speaking into Ali Baba's ear) You know of a secret way into the palace - around the back - and through your uncle, Ali the hairdresser's, shop?

Genius Let me make sure I've got this right. You go down the back alley - Ali - and past Ali the barber - Ali Baba?
Kaliban Eh? Don't mess about. How much does he charge anyway?
Ali Baba Three pounds for a haircut, two pounds for a shave.
Kaliban Three pounds for a haircut, two pounds for a shave? Hmm. I'll let him shave me head then. Come on, what are we waiting for? Genius, you mind the stall, while Ali shows me this secret entrance. *(to the audience)* He, he! I'm going to steal the Kalandar stone. Yes I am.
Audience No you're not.
Kaliban Oh yes I am.
Audience Oh no you're not.
Ali Baba Can we get on sire? You'll be here all day with that lot. By the way sire, I wonder whether you could let me have something on account?
Kaliban On account of what?
Ali Baba On account of I'm skint at the moment.
Kaliban Huh! No chance. *(as he exits)* Don't boo me when I go off.

Kaliban and Ali Baba exit to boos from the audience

Kaliban *(returning quickly)* I said, don't boo me.

Kaliban exits before the audience has time to reply, and Genius takes up his place behind the stall

Genius Roll up! Roll up! Go potty, buy a pot.

Enter Marco and Omar, who is carrying some papers

Omar Marco, I bet you can't tell me, what goes ha-ha-ha-clonk?
Marco I don't know.
Omar A man laughing his head off!
Marco Huh! I bet you don't know what you get if you cross a slice of toast with a duvet.
Omar No.
Marco Breakfast in bed.
Omar You've been at the Christmas crackers again, haven't you? Look, there's a chap selling pots. Perhaps he'll buy one of my poems. *(to Genius)* Excuse me, would you like to buy one of my poems?
Genius Do you want the long answer or the short answer?
Omar Er, the long answer.
Genius The long answer is no.
Omar Eh? If that's the long answer then what's...
Genius Don't ask, as a rude gesture may give offence. Would you would care to purchase a pot?
Marco What for?
Genius He could put his poems in it, and bury them.
Marco Yes, then they'd be potty, potted poems.
Genius Permanently potted, potty poems, I hope.

Omar You won't laugh when I'm famous.
Marco Come on, let's go to C and A, they've got a sale on.

Exit Marco and Omar, and enter Sinbad and Kashoo

Sinbad Let me buy you something Kashoo.
Kashoo You mustn't keep buying me presents Sinbad.
Sinbad Why not? I like buying you presents.
Kashoo But we must save our money for when we are married.
Sinbad When I return from my next voyage we will be rich. *(going to Ali Baba's stall)* Perhaps I should buy mother a pot.
Kashoo There isn't one big enough to put her in.
Sinbad Now Kashoo, don't be unkind. She's nice really. *(looking at Genius)* Hey, you're not Ali Baba.
Genius That is true. But you are the one known as Sinbad the Sailor.
Sinbad Yes, that's right. How did you know?
Genius You do not remember me sire?
Sinbad No, I don't think so.
Genius Don't you remember your adventure with the fearsome great bird, the Roc?
Kashoo I remember you telling me about that Sinbad.
Sinbad Oh yes, that big ugly thing.
Kashoo You said it reminded you of your mother.
Sinbad Hey wait a minute - I remember now.

Kashoo now groans noisily at the puns, which should be strongly emphasised

You were the one who was imprisoned in the giant Roc's egg. You tried to scramble out. Shell, shell, I tell them about it?
Genius Don't poach my story please. It was no yoke being in there. It was all white for you, getting all egg-cited, but I almost cracked up in there.
Kashoo *(to the audience)* The old jokes are best.
Genius I am gratified that you remember sire.
Sinbad Then what are you doing here?
Genius   Alas, it was my misfortune to cross the path of one Kaliban El Krookid, Kaliph of Kufabad.
Sinbad I say! Try saying that six times quickly!
Genius Yes. We've just done that one sire.
Sinbad Oh, right. So what's old Kali-Kufy-what's-it got to do with it then?
Genius Well, no sooner had you so kindly rescued me from the Roc's egg, than Kaliban imprisoned me in a lamp, which he carries around his neck. I am his prisoner, and must obey his every command.
Sinbad I say, that's jolly bad luck.
Genius It seems my destiny is to be forever in tight spots.
Sinbad Better than being forever in spotty tights I suppose.
Genius If you say so sire. I am grateful for what you tried to do for me, and I would like to repay my debt to you.
Sinbad Hey! You're going to offer me three wishes, aren't you?

Kashoo I hope he is. Let me see now, First I would like a nice new...
Genius Alas no sire. That's a completely different pantomime you see.
Kashoo (disappointed) Pity.
Genius I may only grant wishes to the one who holds the lamp you see.
Kashoo We understand.
Genius I can do something for you. I can tell you you are in great danger.
Kashoo Great danger?
Sinbad (to Kashoo) Mother must be in a temper again.
Genius Worse than that.
Sinbad Worse than mother in a temper? It must be bad.
Genius Soon a great calamity will befall the town. But I will use my powers to
see that it does not affect you.

Enter Widow Duffcake

Widow Duffcake There you are! What are you doing?
Sinbad Not now mother.
Widow Duffcake Don't you "not now mother" me! I sent you out to get the
Sultan some breakfast cereal, and you've been gone ages.
Sinbad Mother, there's a disaster about to happen.
Widow Duffcake Yes. if the Sultan doesn't get his breakfast.
Kashoo No! Listen to Genius here.
Widow Duffcake Genius! He doesn't look like much of a genius to me.
Genius Shall I turn her into a frog Sinbad?
Kashoo Turn her into a human being would be better.
Sinbad He's a magic genie from a container.
Widow Duffcake I see. He tells you there's a magic genie in every container,
so you buy one.
Genius (concentrating hard) WAIT! It's happening!
Widow Duffcake (looking round) What? Where?
Genius Yes, yes! It's about to happen!
Widow Duffcake Well control yourself - we don't want it happening here.
Genius Kaliban has infiltrated the palace.
Widow Duffcake (beginning to panic, and pacing up and down the stage)
Kaliban has fumigated the palace.
Genius The Sultan is betrayed.
Widow Duffcake The Sultan is depraved.
Genius He's in a nasty fix.
Widow Duffcake He can't find his Weetabix.

*Light begins to dim, distant flashing lights and thunder rolls, gradually
building in intensity. The chorus move about in panic. Some may exit*

Sinbad Oh no!
Widow Duffcake They've got the weather forecast wrong again. They never
said anything about this. I'll kill that Michael Fish!
Genius The stone is taken, without a doubt!
Widow Duffcake My nightie is ruined, I've left the washing out!

Genius The people are falling into a deep slumber.
Widow Duffcake I'm turning into a cheap cucumber.

The lightning and thunder rolls rise to a climax with a final loud crash

Genius The deed is done.
Widow Duffcake I want me mum.

All on stage, except Sinbad and Genius, are frozen like statues

A calm descends upon the stage. The flashes and thunder die out

Genius Alas. The stone is now Kaliban's.
Sinbad Good heavens!
Genius What is it?
Sinbad Look at mother! It's the first time she's been quiet in years.

Widow Duffcake's eyes move in a glare towards Sinbad, and her expression turns to anger, but she remains frozen

Genius Sinbad, a great disaster has befallen your city.
Sinbad We must do something. You're not going to leave poor Kashoo like that are you? Can't you wake her up?
Genius Well perhaps I could work my magic on one more. As I owe you a favour. Who is it to be, your mother, or Kashoo?
Sinbad *(not sure)* Well...

Sinbad looks at both of them. When attention is on her somehow Widow Duffcake manages to get her finger to point to herself, together with some eyebrow movements, and an over-sweet smile, that indicates that she thinks it should be her

(looking at his mother) I think mother is trying to tell me something. What is it Genius?

Widow Duffcake manages to nod

Genius *(concentrating again)* Yes, there is a message coming through...
Sinbad What is she saying?
Genius A boy's best friend is his mother. And - wait a minute, something else - I'll kill you when I get hold of you.

Widow Duffcake nods again

Sinbad *(turning to the audience)* Charming! Perhaps these people can help me. Who should I wake up?

The audience will give different answers

(pointing to Kashoo) Kashoo?

The audience will respond again with "Yes", *and* "No"

(pointing to Widow Duffcake) Mother?

Again, similar responses from the audience

Genius Kaliban will be here in a minute Sinbad. Decide quickly.
Sinbad I'll put it to the vote. *(to Genius)* Have you got a shoutometer?

As Sinbad addresses the audience. Genius exits and brings on a giant thermometer, the "mercury" of which he operates from behind as the audience shouts

When I say mother, shout out "yes" if you want it to be her. Then, when I say Kashoo, shout out "yes" if you want it to be her. Right? Are you ready?
Audience Yes.
Sinbad *(pointing to Widow Duffcake)* Mother?
Audience Yes.
Sinbad *(pointing to Kashoo)* Kashoo?
Audience Yes.
Genius Hurry sire.
Sinbad Right. I've decided - Mother...

Widow Duffcake puts on a big smile

You stay like that.

Widow Duffcake's expression turns to anger

Kashoo is released.

Genius waves his hand and Kashoo relaxes. Widow Duffcake's hand makes a raised fist that shakes gently

Kashoo What happened?
Sinbad Kashoo I've had you released because I need you to help me to get the stone back to its rightful owner.
Kashoo Right Sinbad.
Genius Quick! Kaliban is approaching! Get out of here. *(goes to the magic carpet, seizes it, and gives it to Sinbad)* Take this, you may need it.
Sinbad Does it work?
Genius Of course. It's only had one, careful lady owner. Now go.

Sinbad and Kashoo exit on one side with the carpet. Enter, from the other side, Kaliban with the stone, and Ali Baba

The curtain slowly closes as Genius, Kaliban and Ali Baba move forward in front of tabs, or a frontcloth

Scene 5

A street near the bazaar. As for Scene 3

Kaliban What a triumph! Like taking candy from a kid.
Ali Baba I can see the headlines now, 'Kaliban El Krookid, Kaliph of Kufabad, takes Kandy from Kid'.
Genius Bit of a mouthful isn't it? It'll fill up the whole page.

Kaliban now proceeds to jump about the stage in a very exaggerated fashion, demonstrating how he defeated the enemy

Kaliban You should have seen us. In we went - through the secret entrance that leads to the palace harem - known only to Ali Baba here...
Ali Baba And my three hundred and fifty seven male relatives.
Kaliban In amongst the Sultan's police - swarming everywhere, all seven thousand of them.
Genius Sounds like Chelsea *(or local team)* playing at home.
Kaliban How many guards did I say?
Ali Baba Seven thousand.
Kaliban Make it ten thousand.
Genius Make it twenty thousand - who's counting?
Kaliban Don't exaggerate, please! To the first one I said, "Your money or your life".
Genie What did he say?
Kaliban He said, "Take my life, I'm saving my money for my old age".
Genius Ah! *(to the audience)* The old jokes are best.
Kaliban Then - into the Sultan's harem.
Genius Ooh!
Kaliban Wrong door. Out of the Sultan's harem.
Ali Baba *(slyly to audience)* Back in the Sultan's harem.
Kaliban I wondered where you'd got to.
Ali Baba Oh yes. The Sultan has a wife for every day of the week. I'd just got to Thursday, when suddenly...
Kaliban Out of the harem.
Ali Baba He pulls me out of the harem.
Kaliban Take a glass of Lucozade and...
Ali Baba Back in the harem.
Kaliban Back in the ha... NO! Finally we got to the Executioner, Mesrour.
Ali Baba *(dreamily)* You speak for yourself. I'm still in the harem.

Final section here to be said quickly, accompanied with a frenzy of movement from Kaliban

Kaliban We drew swords. Round and round we went. Cut, thrust. In, out.

Genius *(doing the movements)* Knees bend, arms stretch, ra, ra, ra.
Kaliban Then the palace guards arrived. I fought one here. I fought one there.
Genius And fought one round the corner.
Kaliban Guards to the left of me, guards to the right of me...
Genius Into the valley of death rode the six hundred.
Kaliban Make it seven hundred.
Ali Baba *(yawning)* Make it eight hundred, who cares?
Kaliban Finally, what happened?
Genius You woke up and it was all a dream.
Kaliban I woke up and it was all a... No I didn't.
Genius Oh yes you did.
Kaliban Oh no I didn't. I seized the stone and ran. And here we are. *(holding up the stone)* And here it is.

Kaliban does a "winners lap" of the stage as the music for "Match of the day", or a recording of a cheering football crowd comes up. He finally collapses into the arms of Genius and Ali Baba

Ali Baba Truly wonderful master. *(craftily)* May I presume that we are all on a percentage here?
Kaliban What? You can presume what you like. Let me see now, what's half of er...
Ali Baba *(excited, walking round stage)* HALF! You're going to give us half! How wonderful! I'm rich! RICH! RICH!
Kaliban If you let me finish...
Ali Baba How generous master! I'm going to get half. Half! I never expected so much! How can I ever thank you?
Kaliban Will you let me finish? I was going to say, "What's half of nothing?"
Ali Baba *(suddenly deflated)* Half of nothing?
Genius *(to Ali Baba)* When you know him as well as I do, you'll know not to get excited like that.
Ali Baba *(sadly)* For a brief moment there I felt as rich as the chairman of a privatised water company.
Genius And now you just feel a drip.

Song No 9

A trio from Kaliban, Ali Baba and Genius, "You've got to Pick a Pocket or Two" or "We're in the money" or "Money Makes the World go Around" or another

At the end of the song

Kaliban Here, what are we all standing around in the street for? Genius, take us back to the palace.
Genius Very good master.

Genius waves his hands and the curtains open

Scene 6

The palace harem, as for Scene 2. The curtains open on a deserted stage as Kaliban, Genius and Ali Baba move back. There needs to be a chair, or cushions to place the "sleeper" on

Kaliban That's better. Now bring on the dancing girls.
Genius That will be rather difficult master.
Kaliban Difficult? I'm the boss now. I can do anything I want.
Genius The dancing girls are all turned into a deep sleep.
Kaliban Oh yea, I'd forgotten about that.

Sinbad and Kashoo shuffle slyly on stage unnoticed by Kaliban or Ali Baba, and stand still, trying to listen. Sinbad has the magic carpet under his arm

Genius Perhaps you should rest after all that excitement. You must be exhausted!
Kaliban *(mopping his brow)* I am. It was worse than being at Harrods sale.

Sinbad and Kashoo shuffle nearer

Genius But what about all the people sire? Surely you're not going to leave them just sitting around motionless?
Kaliban Oh just prop them all up in front of a tele, no-one will notice the difference.
Genius That's true.
Kaliban *(suddenly noticing Sinbad and Kashoo)* Here. Wait a minute. I didn't notice them before. Where did they come from?
Genius They are citizens of Baghdad sire. Frozen in sleep since you stole the stone.

Kaliban, Ali Baba and Genius go over to Sinbad and Kashoo, and peer closely at them

Kaliban You sure? I thought I saw this one move.
Genius An illusion sire, I assure you.

Kaliban deliberately turns his back on Sinbad and Kashoo, then turns to them quickly, trying to catch them out

Kaliban *(still not convinced)* Hmm. Got any pepper?

Sinbad looks suddenly worried

Ali Baba What for?
Kaliban I want to stuff some up their noses, see if they sneeze.
Genius *(trying to save the situation)* But sire, you'll have us all sneezing.
Kaliban But it's an opportunity - wait for it - not to be sneezed at! Ha, ha!

Sinbad pulls a face

Ali Baba Who said the old jokes are best?
Kaliban I just made up that joke to see if they'd laugh you see.
Genius You were hoping for a miracle.
Kaliban *(looking at Sinbad very closely)* Did you laugh then?

Sinbad shakes his head

Did you move your head in any way?

Sinbad shakes his head again

You sure?

Sinbad nods

(to the audience) Is he pretending?

Sinbad gives an emphatic shake of his head, and mouths a silent "No" to the audience when Kaliban is not looking

Audience No.
Kaliban Somebody said "Yes". I heard it. Is he pretending?

Again Sinbad implores the audience to say "No"

Audience NO!
Kaliban Alright then. Now Genius, magic us away.
Genius Very good sire. Where do you want me to drop you off?
Kaliban King Harold's Close.
Genius Is he? I'll try and lose him at the traffic-lights master. Will you be travelling first or economy class?
Ali Baba Silly question.
Genius Very well, first class it is.
Kaliban Can we drop you off somewhere Ali? We're going past the reservoir.
Ali Baba Most amusing master.
Kaliban Now I must put the stone in a safe place.
Genius What about your wallet, you never open that?
Kaliban I shall place it in the cave of the - Long-tailed, red-eyed, snake-necked, loud-roaring dragon.

Sinbad and Kashoo look at each other in alarm

Genius and **Ali Baba** *(together, very dramatically)* NO! Not the - Long-tailed, red-eyed, snake-necked, loud-roaring dragon!

Kaliban Yes. The long-tailed... Oh I'm not doing all that again. He will guard it for me. No-one would ever dare to go near him, and I shall rule forever! Genius, I'm a genius! Fly us there.

They begin to exit

Ali Baba And make sure the in-flight movie is The Terminator.
Kaliban Hey! I want to watch the Thief of Baghdad.
Ali Baba What are you talking about? You are the Thief of Baghdad!

As they exit

Genius *(holding his nose)* This is your Captain, Genius of the Lamp, speaking. We are flying at thirty thousand feet. The temperature on the ground is...

When they have gone, Sinbad and Kashoo relax

Sinbad Whew! That was a close shave.
Kashoo I was getting cramp there.
Sinbad We must follow them to the dragon's cave and get the stone back.
Kashoo Roll the magic carpet out then.

Sinbad puts the carpet down near the wings

Sinbad I wish we could do something for mother and the others.

Enter Genius

Genius Sinbad, I've just remembered something that might help.
Sinbad Good. What is it?
Genius It's one of my inventions. My Enlivening Machine.
Kashoo Enlivening Machine! What does that do?
Genius Well it's for those long debates in parliament. You pass people through it, and it keeps them awake.
Kashoo Well let's try it.
Sinbad Yes, if it works on politicians it must be good.

Genius and Sinbad go to the wings and wheel on the Enlivening Machine, which is like an airport metal-detecting walk-through, or two poles on stands, like shop-exit security devices (see production notes)

Genius Here it is. I can't stay long. I hear my master calling.
Kaliban *(off)* GENIUS! COME HERE.
Genius *(calling to off stage)* Coming master. *(to Sinbad)* You must use the magic password though.

Genius begins to exit

Sinbad *(calling after him)* The magic password! Quick, tell us the password!
Kaliban *(off)* GENIUS!
Genius *(calling off stage)* Yes master. I'm on my way. *(to Sinbad)* It must be done to noisy saucepans.

Genius exits

Sinbad Noisy saucepans?
Kashoo He's not winding us up is he?
Sinbad Oh dear, I hope not.
Kashoo Perhaps you bang a saucepan as someone goes through.
Sinbad Mother does that and it only gives me a headache.
Kashoo Well, perhaps you say "saucepans" as you pass them through.
Sinbad Let's try it.

They go to the wings and carry on a sleeping Omar, who is cuddling a giant Teddy Bear. They take him through the machine, calling out, "saucepans" as they go. Omar remains asleep, and they place him on the chair

Kashoo That's no good.
Sinbad Hang on. Genius said, "noisy saucepans". Perhaps we didn't say it loud enough.
Kashoo *(indicating the audience)* Perhaps we can get these people to help us.
Sinbad Yes. Will you help us?
Audience Yes.
Kashoo Will you shout out, "saucepans", when we put him through?
Audience Yes.
Sinbad Right, as loud as you can. Let's try again.

They repeat the process of carrying Omar through the machine. The audience shouts out "saucepans". A loud hooter sounds, and Omar comes to life

Omar *(talking to the Teddy Bear)* Sometimes I ask the question, does it seem, as though this life is nothing but a dream?
Kashoo He's back to normal!
Sinbad You call that normal? How do we get him back to sleep again?
Omar What happened?
Kashoo Never mind that now. Help Sinbad with Marco.

Sinbad and Omar bring Marco on wearing football strip, Kashoo gets audience to shout "saucepans". Marco goes through machine, hooter sounds. He wakes

Marco I was dreaming that England's football team won the World Cup then.
Omar and **Sinbad** *(sing)* "To dream the impossible dream!"
Sinbad Now we fetch mother.

Sinbad and Omar go and carry on a sleeping Widow Duffcake, dressed in a night cap, colourful nightie and bloomers. They take her over to the machine

Widow Duffcake *(talking in her sleep)* No Kevin no. Put me down Kevin.

Sinbad *(hesitating before passing her through)* Kevin? Who's Kevin? Are you sure this is a good idea?

Kashoo You've got to face the music sometime. *(to audience)* Don't forget to shout out "saucepans" very loud.

They take Widow Duffcake through the machine as Kashoo encourages the audience to shout out. The loud hooter sounds again, and Widow Duffcake comes to life

Widow Duffcake Here! Put me down! What do you think you're doing? Oh I must have dozed off there for a moment. Waking me up like that! Now I'll never know what Kevin Kostner was saying to me.

Kashoo *(to Sinbad)* There's nothing wrong with her.

Widow Duffcake YES! That's what he was saying to me!

Kashoo He needs a good optician then.

Sinbad I said this machine wasn't a good idea. Mother, you and Omar get the others through this contraption. We've got to go into the dragon's cave and get the stone back.

Widow Duffcake *(up and down the stage)* Oh! The dragon's cave! Help! My poor boy! Be careful! Oh, he's going to be eaten by the horrible dragon!

Sinbad Come on Kashoo.

Kashoo Yes. I'd sooner face the dragon.

Widow Duffcake Oh! Dragon! I wish they wouldn't keep saying that. He's doomed, doomed! And what's to become of me? I'll be an orphan! Help!

Sinbad She needs a tranquilliser dart.

Kashoo She needs an elephant gun.

Song No 10

A quintet; Widow Duffcake, Sinbad, Kashoo, Omar and Marco sing "Wish me Luck as you Wave me Good-bye" or "High Hopes" or another

At the end of the song, Kashoo and Sinbad kneel on the carpet. A spot comes up on the carpet, and all the other lights go down

Sinbad Take us to the dragon's cave.

Wind sounds come up, lights flash

Kashoo We're flying!

Sinbad It really works!

Fade spot

Curtain

End of Act 1

Act 2

Scene 1

The curtains open on the cave of the dragon. It is a deserted, eerie, gloomy place, cast in a green light and strewn with debris, giant bones etc., Notices are displayed saying, "Keep out, by order of the dragon" etc., There should be somewhere for Sinbad and Kashoo to sit amongst the debris, that still leaves room for the dancers - a seat on the apron will do. Also needed is somewhere for Eric to hide, unless the wings are used

When the scene has established itself, a group of mini-dragons enter

Music No. 11

A junior chorus number. To an appropriate piece of music, "The Firebird Suite" or "Hall of the Mountain King" or "March of the Siamese Children" or another, the mini-dragons dance. This may be a dance performed under a fluorescent light, if desired, for added effect

At the end of the dance the dancers exit

A moment later, Sinbad and Kashoo fall in through the wings. The carpet is ....

Sinbad Well, thanks very much! Next time I'll book with Thomas Cook!
Kashoo Didn't you put the hand brake on?
Sinbad Hand brake? Of course not!
Kashoo Why not?
Sinbad Because it's not been invented yet.
Kashoo Oh. This must be the dragon's cave. Horrible isn't it?
Sinbad I've just remembered something.
Kashoo What's that?.
Sinbad I've forgotten to bring anything to fight the dragon with.
Kashoo Great! I'm glad you've remembered you've forgotten to remember.
Sinbad Kashoo! Don't get me confused! I'll just have to fight him with my bare hands.

Sinbad looks around the stage

Kashoo It's spooky, isn't it?
Sinbad There's no one in. I hope he's been made redundant.
Kashoo Let's hope he's not hungry if he comes back.

Kashoo and Sinbad sit down

Sinbad I wonder how big this dragon is.
Kashoo I'm told he is fantastically huge, and very fierce.
Sinbad Well thanks for cheering me up. *(stands up and addresses the audience)* Ladies and Gentlemen, since this adventure is going to be very dangerous, I'd like to receive my applause in advance. Thank you.

He encourages the audience to applaud. Kashoo pulls a face, and laughs at him. Then, not satisfied with the amount of applause, Sinbad appeals to them again

Can't you do better than that? I could get murdered here!

He encourages the audience to applaud louder. Then, still not satisfied

Huh! I'm not getting eaten by a dragon for that!

He begins to exit, but Kashoo calls him back

Kashoo Come back here. You're not really scared, are you?

Sinbad sits down

Sinbad *(not very convincingly)* No. Of course not.

Eric, the Ghostly Echo of the cave, enters behind them

Kashoo *(indicating the audience)* These people will tell us if anything tries to sneak up on us, won't you?
Audience It's behind you.

Eric hides as Sinbad and Kashoo get up and look around

Sinbad There's nothing there.
Kashoo *(to audience)* Where was it?

Eric appears again when they are facing the front

Audience Behind you.

Eric hides again, as Sinbad and Kashoo look again

Sinbad I can't see anything.
Kashoo *(to audience)* Was it the dragon?

Confused replies from the audience, as Eric appears again and comes up close behind them. Sinbad and Kashoo sit still and face the front

Sinbad I don't think there's anything there.
Kashoo *(to audience)* You shouldn't try to frighten us like that.

Sinbad I wasn't frightened anyway.

Eric is now peering out between their heads, and the audience will be yelling at them to look round

Kashoo *(to audience)* Is it there again?
Audience Yes.
Kashoo *(to Sinbad)* Do you think we should look round?
Sinbad No. There's nothing there.

To a crash, Eric puts his hands on their shoulders, and they freeze, with eyes wide and mouths open

Kashoo I think it's time to look round Sinbad.
Sinbad Yes, I think it's time to look round Kashoo.

Sinbad and Kashoo slowly look round. Then they jump, to another crash, as they see Eric

Eric Hello.
Sinbad and **Kashoo** *(together)* Er, hello,
Eric I hope I didn't frighten you?
Sinbad *(moping his brow)* Oh no, of course not.
Kashoo What kind of dragon are you?
Eric I'm not a dragon.
Sinbad Then who are you, and what are you doing in here?
Eric *(now sitting between them)* I am the Ghostly Echo of the cave. My friends call me Eric.
Kashoo Eric?
Eric Yes. Eric. It stands for - Echo Revolving In Cave. Clever, isn't it? I thought it up myself. I used to be a civil servant, in an earlier life you see. We went in for that sort of thing a lot.
Kashoo And do you have many friends?
Eric Not really. I frighten most of them away.
Sinbad I'm not surprised.
Kashoo So, why aren't you doing your echoing thing now then?
Eric It's my lunch break.
Kashoo Oh.
Eric I could give you a sample if you like.
Kashoo Oh alright. Go on then.
Eric It's all done by the arms you see. *(waves arms)* When I wave them everything echoes around.

An echo reverberates around the cave, gradually fading out

Echo Echoes around. Echoes around. Echoes around.
Kashoo I say! That's jolly clever.
Sinbad Where did you learn to do that?

Eric Evening classes at *(local college)*. It's something to do now I'm retired.

Eric waves his arms and the echo goes round the cave again

Echo I'm retired. I'm retired. I'm retired.
Eric I got this part-time job for the dragon. You've got to take what you can get, haven't you? I don't enjoy it very much. *(waves arms again)* I'm supposed to frighten people away.
Echo People away. People away. People away.
Eric *(waving arms)* It's very lonely work. We don't get many visitors here.
Echo Visitors here. Visitors here. Visitors here.
Sinbad Well you wouldn't, would you, not with you doing that, and a dragon around?
Kashoo No. It's not exactly Alton Towers?

Eric waves his arms as Kashoo is speaking, and the echo now picks up her words

Echo Alton Towers. Alton Towers.
Kashoo Hey! You made me do it then. *(shouts)* ALTON TOWERS.
Echo No more free advertising please.
Eric Oh yes, it's quite an advanced system, digital sound and everything.

The roar of the dragon comes up

Sinbad Oh! That's clever Eric. How did you do that?
Eric That wasn't me. That's the dragon returning from his morning stroll.
Kashoo Oh er...

Sinbad and Kashoo get up. The dragon roars again

Eric Yes. He likes to build up a healthy appetite for lunch.
Sinbad I wonder what's on the menu?
Eric You are, I think. *(rising)* I must go. The dragon doesn't like me talking to his food, I mean, to his visitors. Good-bye. It was nice chatting to you.

Eric exits. The dragon roars. A huge shadow of a dragon's head appears on the back of the cave. Sinbad and Kashoo wait, terrified

Sinbad Perhaps, if we ask him nicely, he'll let us have the stone back?

The dragon roars louder

Kashoo He's getting closer.

As the roar reaches a climax, and Sinbad and Kashoo stand rigid. There is a crash, and one of the mini-dragons enters. The roars fade out

Sinbad Is that it?
Kashoo Not very big, is it?
Sinbad I didn't care how big it was really. I wasn't frightened of a silly dragon.
Kashoo No, I could tell that by the way your teeth were chattering.
Sinbad I'll soon polish this little blighter off. Then we can search for the stone.

Sinbad begins to advance on the mini-dragon. The mini-dragon begins to cry, and holds out his hand

Kashoo Wait a minute Sinbad. He's upset.
Sinbad He'll be more upset when I've strangled him.
Kashoo *(going over to the mini-dragon)* Look. He's fallen over and cut his hand.
Sinbad Are you going to let me strangle him or not?
Kashoo *((giving the mini-dragon a cuddle)* You can't hurt him. He's a sweet little thing, aren't you?

Mini-dragon nods his head. Kashoo takes him over to the seat, sits him down, and looks at his hand

Sinbad Kashoo! We've come here to kill him, not turn him into a pet. You'll be taking him for a walk in the park next.
Kashoo Oh, that's a good idea! *(to Mini-dragon)* Show me your poor hand then.

Kashoo takes out a handkerchief and bandages the hand up

There now. Is that better?

Mini-dragon nods his head. The dragon roars, off stage, again

Sinbad He did that without moving his lips!
Kashoo Is that your daddy?

Mini-dragon nods again. The shadow of the dragon's head appears on the cave wall again, and the roar comes closer

Sinbad He's a ventriloquist!
Kashoo You'd better go to your daddy then.

Mini-dragon rises to go. To a crash, the Dragon enters with a roar and charges around the stage, stopping opposite the group, and bearing down on them. Sinbad and Kashoo back away. The Dragon roars

Sinbad Stone the crows!
Kashoo What were you saying about not being afraid, no matter how big he was?

Mini-dragon goes over to him and shows him the bandage. The dragon looks at it. Mini-dragon points to Kashoo

Sinbad I bet you don't want to take the big one for a walk in the park.

The dragon makes a small roar, and shakes his head

Kashoo We could always make a run for it.
Echo *(off)* He's saying thank you.
Sinbad *(looking round)* It's Eric.

Dragon roars again

Kashoo *(looking up)* What's he saying now Eric?
Echo He wants to give you a reward.

Dragon nods his head

Sinbad I say, that's a bit of luck. Ask him not to eat us.
Kashoo I'll ask him for the stone. *(going over to the Dragon)* Do you think you could let us have the magic stone back please? It's been stolen by that horrible Kaliban, you see, and everyone's been cruelly put to sleep, and our friends can't get married until it's returned.

The Dragon wanders around the stage

Echo He's thinking about it.
Sinbad Thank you Eric.

Finally the Dragon stops and nods

Kashoo Can we really?

Dragon nods again

Echo Better take it and go, before he changes his mind.
Sinbad But we don't know where it is.
Kashoo Can you tell us where it is then please?

Dragon roars again

Sinbad Eric! Can you interpret for us?
Eric One of his children has it.
Kashoo Oh. Are there more? Can we see them all then?

Dragon roars again, and enter the other mini-dragons, one of whom has the stone. This is handed to Kashoo

Sinbad and **Kashoo** *(together)* Thank you very much.

The Dragon roars

Eric He says you can't go yet.
Sinbad Oh dear. I don't like the sound of that. He's not getting hungry is he?
Eric No. He wants to sing a song.
Kashoo Oh, that's alright then.

Enter, running, Widow Duffcake, brandishing a rolling-pin, or umbrella, Raisin and Kalandar Prince

Widow Duffcake *(running round the stage)* We're all here. Dragon, come out wherever you are! I'll kill you! Where is he? What have you done with my poor boy? Duffcake will duff you up.
Sinbad I'm here mother. It's alright, we're safe.
Widow Duffcake *(very agitated)* Oh son! How you must have suffered! Tell your poor mother all about it.
Kashoo Don't carry on. You'll frighten the poor dragon.
Sinbad Mother we've got the stone. Now we must get it back to the Sultan.
Prince And sort Kaliban out.

Everyone exchanges relieved glances. Enter Omar and Marco, armed to the teeth with bows, arrows, shields, swords, guns, armour etc.,

Omar and **Marco** *(together)* We're here. You're safe now.
Raisin You're just in time to be too late.
Widow Duffcake Wait a minute. You mean the dragon didn't want to eat you?
Sinbad No mother.
Widow Duffcake *(going over to the dragon)* Why not? What's wrong with my boy then eh? He's just as good to eat as anyone else you know.
Sinbad Mother!
Widow Duffcake I'm not having him picking on you like that.

Enter Eric

Eric Good luck.
Raisin Who's that?
Sinbad That's my friend, Eric the Echo.
Prince Eric the Echo?
Sinbad I'll explain it all later.

Song No. 12

A song sung by all on stage, "When you've got friends" or "Consider Yourself One of Us" or "Fortuosity" or another

At the end of the song

Sinbad *(to the Kalandar Prince)* Prince Ahmed, here is your stone restored to you.
Prince *(taking the stone)* Thank you for your help Sinbad. You and Kashoo have been very brave. But now there is another danger for us to face together. We must go to Kufabad and arrest Kaliban.
Sinbad Lead on Prince.
Omar *(indicating Marco and himself)* Include us.
Marco Sure thing.
Prince Raisin, I give you this stone to guard, and return to your father.
Raisin We will do as you wish Ahmed.

The dragon roars

Eric He says, 'call again'.
Kashoo No thanks. He might not be in such a good mood next time. *(to the mini-dragons)* Good-bye.

Everyone waves as Widow Duffcake etc., exit, leaving Dragon, mini-dragons, and Eric on stage

The curtain slowly closes

Scene 2

On the way to Kufabad Castle. This can be played in front of tabs, or a frontcloth showing a mountain pass, or the outside of a castle

Enter Omar and Marco

Marco It takes it out of you, this exploring lark.
Omar Not exactly Harrison Ford, are you? You need a poem to liven you up?
Marco Er, no I don't think so.
Omar You know, your trouble is you're not positive, definite enough.
Marco Alright, I positively, definitely, don't want one of your poems.
Omar Oh. You're not very good at adventuring, are you?
Marco Yes I am. I'm going to be a frogman.
Omar Well, you've got the legs for it.
Marco Omar, what's black and comes out of the desert shouting, Knickers, knickers, knickers?
Omar I don't know.
Marco Crude oil!
Omar Oh. I bet you don't know this one. Why do camels have long necks?
Marco I don't know. Why do camels have long necks?
Omar To join their heads to their bodies, stupid.
Marco You're stupid.
Omar Who said?
Marco I did.

Omar I want a second opinion.
Marco Alright, you're ugly as well. I bet you don't even know this. What do you call a man with a jelly in one ear, and custard in the other?
Omar I don't know.
Marco You call him, "a trifle deaf!" HA, HA!

Enter Sinbad and Prince Ahmed

Prince We're nearly there. Now men. We must use the element of surprise to our advantage. Burst in on him, before he has time to defend himself.
Sinbad Right.
Prince Gather round. I've got a plan all worked out.

They huddle, secretively, round Prince Ahmed, looking round to make sure they are not being overheard

Sinbad Right. Tell us the plan then.
Prince *(looking round)* Shh. Right. The plan is this.

They look round again, and huddle together. Omar sneezes. The rest jump

Sinbad What was that?
Omar Only me.
Prince Shh! Now, where were we?
Omar *(looking round)* Shh.
Marco You were going to tell us the plan.
Prince Oh yes.

Prince looks round again and they go into another huddle

Omar WILL YOU GET ON WITH IT!
Prince SHH!
Marco, Sinbad and **Omar** *(together)* SHH!
Prince Right. Pay attention. This is very important.
Omar We'll be here all night!
Sinbad, Prince and **Marco** *(together)* SHH!
Sinbad Ahmed, will you please tell us the plan?

They all look round again and go into a huddle

Prince Oh right. It's quite simple really. All the best plans are. We just rush through the front door and grab him.

Omar, Sinbad and Marco look dumbfounded for a moment, while Ahmed looks pleased with himself

Sinbad That's the plan?
Omar That really is simple.

Prince Yes. Well, we might have to modify it, of course, if we meet something unexpected.

Sinbad Come on, let's go. It's a comfort to think that the ladies will be safely home by now.

They all exit

Enter Widow Duffcake, carrying a rolling-pin, or baseball-bat

Widow Duffcake Oh no we're not! Come along girls. This way. *(to audience)* Well, you didn't think we were going to let them out on their own did you? *(lifts her skirt and tucks bat into her sock, and hobbles about)* I might need this later.

Enter Kashoo and Raisin,

Raisin *(watching Widow Duffcake hobble around)* She looks like Long John Silver.

Kashoo She never remembers which pantomime she's supposed to be in.

Widow Duffcake *(doing imitation of Long John)* Aha! Come on me hearties. All aboard for Treasure Island! Doubloons and pieces of eight! Aha!

Raisin Here endeth the preview for next year's panto.

They all walk across the stage, Widow Duffcake hobbling, and exit, following in the direction of the men

Scene 3

The banqueting hall of the castle at Kufabad. A table and chairs are centre stage, at which Kaliban sits, drinking. There is a distinctive bottle on the table. Genius is standing in attendance upon him with a jug full of beer

Kaliban Lord of all I survey. This is the life eh Genius?

Genius Yes master.

Kaliban More beer Genius.

Genius Yes master.

Genius pours more beer from the jug

Kaliban *(holding up the bottle from the table)* Now you won't forget to give this bottle of oil to the vet when he arrives, will you?

Genius No master.

Kaliban It's for rubbing on the camel. He's got a bad leg. *(sniffs the bottle)* Whew! It smells horrible.

Genius What's it made from?

Kaliban It's oil of bat-droppings, and ground snake-skins.

Genius No wonder it stinks. With that on, I'd want to run about as well.

Enter Ali Baba, who picks up the "camel oil" bottle

Ali Baba I'm thirsty. I need a drink. *(sniffs the bottle)* Hmm. Smells alright.
Kaliban *(to Genius)* He's not going to, is he?

Kaliban and Genius watch him, then look at each other. They watch him pour some of the oil into a glass and drink it. With his mouth full of liquid his expression changes, and he looks for somewhere to spit the liquid out. He goes to the apron and leans over the audience

Genius Go on then. I dare you.

Ali swallows the liquid

Ali Baba Er! That tasted horrible. Worse than school dinners.
Kaliban You fool! It took three hundred and fifty five bats, and seventeen cobras to produce that!
Genius Now we'll have to rub the camel down with beer!
Ali Baba You could have poisoned me! You know what you'd get for that?
Kaliban Yes, a medal. Never mind, at least the camel will smell good - better than him anyway! It's six o'clock Genius. Time for the news.
Genius Very well. *(hand to brow, concentrating hard)* The time is now six o'clock
Kaliban Do it properly.
Genius Oh, do I have to? I feel such a fool.
Ali Baba That's because you are a fool.
Kaliban Do the news properly I said.
Genius I'll do it properly if you both promise not to laugh.
Kaliban *(stifling a laugh)* No, no. We won't laugh, will we Ali?
Ali Baba *(keeping a straight face with difficulty)* Oh no, of course not.
Genius Alright then. So long as you promise not to laugh.

Genius, protesting, goes to the table and picks up a cut-out of a television set. He looks through the space, at which Ali Baba and Kaliban roar with laughter.

Ali Baba What do you get if you cross a Genie with a TV?
Kaliban I don't know.
Ali Baba SMELLYVISION! HA, HA!
Genius You said you wouldn't laugh! I hate pantomimes.
Ali Baba How do you switch him off? He looks just like that bloke on telly.
Kaliban Which one?
Ali Baba Frankenstein!
Kaliban Get on with it, will you.
Genius *(looking through the television space)* Here is the latest news. In France Charlemagne has been declared Emperor, and the French farmers have asked for more subsidies for their crops, or they will go on strike.
Ali Baba Nothing new there then.

Genius On the Eastern Front Genghis Khan is moving into China with his troops. We bring you this special report from Kate Adie...

Kaliban Yes, yes. Never mind about all that. What about the local news?

Genius Very well. Don't let me finish will you? I wish I'd taken that offer from the BBC.

Ali Baba So do I.

Kaliban Genius, get on with it!

Genius Very well. Here is the local news. Sultan Shahriar, and most of his palace are still slumbering from the mysterious illness that has swept the country. A spokesman for the Medical Council said today...

Kaliban Wait a minute, wait a minute. You said most of the palace?

Genius Oh! I bet Jeremy Paxman doesn't have this trouble.

Kaliban I'll kill him in a minute!

Ali Baba Who, Jeremy Paxman? He's not that bad.

Genius Oh yes he is.

Kaliban Will you tell me what you meant about only most of the palace being asleep. They should all be asleep.

Genius We apologise to our viewers for the interference. Not all of the palace residents are asleep. Some of them seem to have found a way of waking up.

Kaliban and **Ali Baba** *(suddenly alert)* WHAT?

Genius *(all innocence)* I can't think what could have happened.

Ali Baba Something smells here.

Genius Yes. It's you.

Kaliban Will you shut up!

Genius OK. I'll shut up. So you don't want the most interesting piece of news?

Kaliban I'll cut off his Channel 4 in a minute! What's the other news?

Genius Some of them are even now outside your castle. Intent on revenge.

Ali Baba and **Kaliban** *(jumping up)* WHAT?

Kaliban Now wait a minute, I don't want anyone to panic. I want you to walk out of here slowly and casual. You got that?

Ali Baba Slow and casual. Right master.

Ali Baba, Kaliban and Genius half get up slowly, then suddenly make a mad rush for the wings. Kaliban stops

Kaliban Come back here you useless pair of cowards.

Ali Baba and Genius return, obviously scared. They hide behind Kaliban

Will you get off me? Summon the guards!

Castle guards enter

Stand by to defend our person with your lives - or vice versa!

The guards stand at alert, with scimitars or spears at the ready. Kaliban and Ali Baba draw scimitars. All stand to one side to allow the others to enter in front of them

Enter Prince Ahmed, Sinbad, Omar and Marco on tiptoe, fingers on lips, making 'shh' sounds to the audience. They do not see the others and are immediately surrounded, from behind, by Kaliban, Ali Baba, and the guards

Kaliban You are under arrest.
Sinbad Oh great!
Omar *(to Prince Ahmed)* The element of surprise really worked well, didn't it?
Marco Just creep in through the front door and grab him, you said.
Omar He's about as good at tactics as an English football manager.
Prince The plan needed a little modification.
Sinbad It's too late now.
Kaliban Silence! Lock them up. I will question them later.
Ali Baba I'll see to it master.

The prisoners are taken away by the guards, led by Ali Baba

Kaliban Now, Genius, I want you to give me a report from the dragon's cave.
Genius *(nervously)* Er, the dragon's cave master?
Kaliban I want to know if the stone's safe. You didn't mention it on the news.
Genius Oh, that dragon's cave.
Kaliban Well, get on with it! Before I put you back in the lamp, you useless good for nothing!
Genius *(concentrating hard)* Oh dear! *(to audience)* I can't tell him the truth, can I? He'll know it was me that helped Sinbad.
Kaliban What are you mumbling about?
Genius Er, I can't get through master. I'm trying.
Kaliban You are, very trying.
Genius All lines are down master. The power must be cut off.
Kaliban It's not the only things that's going to be cut off! Your head's next. You'd better get over there and find out what's happening.
Genius But that could take some time master.
Kaliban Well I don't need you here. The criminals are safely locked up, and nothing's going to happen here.
Genius *(slyly to audience)* That's what he thinks.
Kaliban Well go on then.
Genius Going master.

Genius exits, and Ali Baba returns

Enter Widow Duffcake, hobbling, Kashoo and Raisin. They are all heavily veiled

Kaliban Who're you? *(to Ali Baba)* It's not Karaoke night again, is it? What's this lot doing here?

Ali Baba I don't know master.

Widow Duffcake We are the new dancers for the harem, your disgracefulness.

Kaliban Dancers? Blimey, this ugly one can hardly walk! She looks like Long John Silver.

Raisin and **Kashoo** *(together)* We've just done that one stupid.

Kaliban Oh. I didn't order any new dancers did I Ali?

Ali Baba I don't think so master.

Kaliban Well I suppose a few more won't hurt. I can afford it.

Widow Duffcake Nothing is too good for you, your baldness.

Raisin Perhaps you would show us where we can prepare ourselves for our exotic dance.

Kaliban Exotic dance eh! I can't wait to see that. Show them where to change Ali.

Ali Baba Yes master.

Ali Baba is about to escort them off. Widow Duffcake bends down to fix the bat in her sock. Kaliban's eye falls upon Widow Duffcake's rear

Kaliban Wait. I will speak with this one alone.

Ali Baba Which one?

Kaliban This big ugly one here.

Widow Duffcake Oh! Here we go again. What it is to be irresistible!

Ali Baba Very well master.

Raisin and Kashoo exit. Ali Baba remains near the wings, cups his hand to his ear, and tries to overhear

Kaliban *(seeing him)* Alone!

Ali Baba Oh, very well. *(to audience, as he exits)* Rotten spoilsport!

Kaliban *(coming close to her)* Tell me, have we not met before?

Widow Duffcake *(moving away)* Oh no your nastiness.

Kaliban *(trying to peer into her veil)* Your face seems familiar. I associate you somehow with...

Widow Duffcake Watch it! I'm not that sort of girl.

Kaliban With diamonds...

Widow Duffcake Oh yes, I'm that sort of girl!

Kaliban Diamond brand saucepans I mean. And with cooking. Why is that?

Widow Duffcake Oh, I can't think.

Kaliban When I look at you I hear pans being banged. Why is that?

Widow Duffcake Oh no! Your unmentionableness. Some nasty person has been making allegations, and if I catch the alligators I'll...

Kaliban That is a beautiful dress.

Widow Duffcake Yes, a man in the village runs up it for me.

Kaliban Ah, you mean, 'runs it up for you'.

Widow Duffcake *(slyly to audience)* Yes of course, how silly of me.

Kaliban Are you the one they call Hopalong Cassidy?

Widow Duffcake Oh no, I'm more of a Linda Lusardi really.

Kaliban Really, you could have fooled me. *(coming close again)* What is your name, my little flower of the desert?
Widow Duffcake *(pushing him away)* Orchid.
Kaliban Orchid?
Widow Duffcake Yes, Desert Orchid. You should see me run.

She makes as if to exit, but is restrained by Kaliban

Kaliban Stay a little longer.
Widow Duffcake I must go, I'm going to the museum.
Kaliban Ah, to be carbon-dated?
Widow Duffcake Oh no! I don't accept dates from strangers. I want to see the dinosaurs.
Kaliban Well keep on the move, they might be stocktaking.
Widow Duffcake Oh you say the sweetest things. *(kicks him)*
Kaliban Ouch! Let me take you to some far off sanctuary...
Widow Duffcake Oh! Sanct-you-ary much!
Kaliban I'm very big round here you know.
Widow Duffcake I wasn't going to mention it. *(looking behind him)* You're pretty big round there too!
Kaliban Oh yes. I've got hidden assets. They call me the boss you know.
Widow Duffcake Who do?
Kaliban The people who work for me, you silly old bat. Oh yes, I've got that indefinable something.
Widow Duffcake Really? What's that?
Kaliban I don't know. It's indefinable, isn't it?
Widow Duffcake Whatever it is, it should be dug in round the rhubarb.
Kaliban *(putting his arm round her)* You are just what I need to brighten up my dark days.
Widow Duffcake *(escaping)* It's not the days I'm worried about.
Kaliban My little pomegranate.
Widow Duffcake Don't! You give me the pip!
Kaliban Come with me to the Kasbar.
Widow Duffcake Which bar?
Kaliban The Kas-bar.
Widow Duffcake Mine's a gin and tonic! Oh! I've never been out with a Kaliban before. A few Wallies and a couple of Charlies, but...
Kaliban *(grabbing her)* Give me a small token.
Widow Duffcake *(escaping)* A gift token? He thinks I'm the Chemist - Boots!
Kaliban She looks more like Rugby boots from here. *(grabbing her)* Give me something to remember you by.
Widow Duffcake *(escaping)* Huh! you'll be lucky. Ooh, it's like wrestling an octopus!
Kaliban WHAT? Summon the guards!
Widow Duffcake Oh no! Alright. I'll give you something to remember.
Kaliban Oh good.

Widow Duffcake   Never trust an electrician with no eyebrows!   Can you remember that?

Kaliban What?

Widow Duffcake And here's something else to remember.

Kaliban What's that?

Widow Duffcake Never scratch your nose at an auction.

Kaliban No. I might end up buying an old antique like you.

Widow Duffcake There's still a few tunes to be played on this antique mate,

Kaliban *(grabbing her again)* Oh you tantalising creature!

Widow Duffcake *(to audience)* I think I've just kissed a frog!

Song No 13

A duet from Kaliban and Widow Duffcake. "Kiss me Honey, Honey" or "Anything You Can Do, I Can Do Better" or "Don't Throw Bouquets at Me" or another. This should be accompanied by a frenetic dance routine, in which Widow Duffcake hobbles about. Alternatively this could be a solo from Widow Duffcake, "Big Spender" or another

At the end of the dance

Widow Duffcake Now take me to the others.

Kaliban Of course. This way.

Widow Duffcake No peeping now, you naughty boy. *(she turns away from him, taking the bat out as she exits)* Is he in for a surprise!

They exit and, in a moment, loud crashes off stage, and cries from Kaliban

Kaliban *(off stage)* Ouch! What do you think you're doing? Let me go!

Enter Widow Duffcake, Raisin and Kashoo

Raisin That's got those two locked up.

Widow Duffcake Well done girls.

Kashoo Now, let's find the men.

They exit

Kaliban *(off)* Genius! Where are you, you fool! Get me out of here!

Enter Genius, to a crash and a flash

Genius I hear my master calling. *(looking round)* I wonder where he is? *(to audience)* Do you know where he is?

Varied responses from audience

Locked up?

Audience Yes.

Genius Really? How wonderful! I mean, oh how terrible. Oh dear. I don't know what to do now. I should go and rescue him really. Shall I do that?
Audience No.
Genius He'll punish me if I don't.

Enter Widow Duffcake, Kashoo, Raisin, Prince Ahmed, Sinbad, Marco and Omar

Sinbad Ah there you are Genius.
Genius Sinbad. I've done a terrible thing.
Raisin So have we. We've just locked up Kaliban and Ali Baba.
Genius It is my duty to rescue him.
Prince Now wait a minute. Don't be hasty.
Kashoo You want to be free, don't you?
Genius Yes, of course I do.
Prince *(indicating the audience)* They don't want Kaliban to be free, do you?
Audience No.
Prince There, you see.
Genius It's all very well for them. It's me that's going to be punished.
Widow Duffcake Will you leave him there, if we promise to set you free?
Kaliban *(off)* Genius! I'll murder you in a minute! Come here!
Raisin What do you say Genius?
Genius But he still has the lamp. I can never be released while he still has it.
Widow Duffcake We will find a way to get it from him.
Genius But how?
Sinbad I have an idea. You remember that machine that woke us all up?
Genius Yes, but how will that help us?
Sinbad Just bring it on will you?
Genius Very well. It's over here.

Genius and Prince Ahmed go to the wings and bring on the Enlivening Machine

Prince Here it is Sinbad, but I don't see how it can help.

The machine is set up in the centre of the stage, and Sinbad positions himself to demonstrate

Sinbad Now, you remember how we put sleepy people through this way and they woke up?
Kaliban *(off)* Will you get me out of this!
Raisin I don't think we need to wake him up Sinbad.
Prince No.
Widow Duffcake He sounds pretty awake already.
Sinbad No, look. If he goes through the other way. Perhaps the opposite will happen.
Prince You mean, if he goes through awake, the wrong way, he'll fall asleep?
Sinbad Yes.
Raisin *(to Genius)* Will it work?

Genius I don't know. It's never been tried.
Widow Duffcake Our mission - to go where no man has gone before.
Omar Thank you Captain Kirk.
All on stage Beam her up Scotty.
Widow Duffcake OH!
Kashoo Let's go for it.
Sinbad We'll need a loud shout of "saucepans" from the audience. Omar and Marco, you organise that.
Marco Right Sinbad.

Marco and Omar prepare to organise the audience to shout

Omar It's got to be really loud OK?
Audience OK.
Sinbad And the magic stone.
Raisin *(producing the stone)* I've got that here.
Sinbad Good, now you stand on the sleepy side of the Machine Raisin.
Raisin *(taking up her position)* Right.
Genius What about me?
Prince Yes, he'd better not find you here Genius.
Genius I'll go and hide. *(exits)*
Sinbad I think that's everything. Now Ahmed, you and Kashoo let him out.

Prince Ahmed and Kashoo exit

Omar When we say "now".
Marco *(to audience)* A very, very, very, big shout of "saucepans".
Widow Duffcake He called me an old dragon out there you know.
Omar A dragon? Did he mother? I can't think why.
Widow Duffcake Yes. A dragon! Just because I hit him a few times.
Sinbad Do you have any idea what's it's like to come face-to-face with a real, huge, horrible, ugly dragon? To experience the excitement, the thrill, the terror. Do you?

Enter Kaliban, hobbling, heavily bandaged. Everyone's attention is on him

Prince, Omar and **Marco** *(together)* No. But we know a man that does.

Prince Ahmed and Kashoo enter and lead Kaliban over to the 'wrong' side of the machine

Kaliban How dare you lock me up like that! What are all these people doing here? You're all supposed to be asleep.
Prince *(pointing to Raisin)* We've got the magic stone, look.
Raisin *(holding up the stone)* Yes, look.
Kaliban *(peering through the machine at the stone)* Here! That's mine! What are you doing with that? Give it to me!
Raisin You only have to come and get it Kaliban.

Kaliban is about to walk through the machine, but hesitates. Prince and Sinbad get ready to catch Kaliban when he comes through the machine

Omar *(to audience)* Not yet.
Kaliban It's not a trick is it?
Prince Of course not. Come on.

Kaliban goes to the machine, then hesitates again, as Raisin entices him

Omar and **Marco** *(together)* Not yet.
Kaliban You sure?
Raisin *(prepares to put the stone away)* Well, if you don't want it.
Kaliban Yes I do. It's mine.
Widow Duffcake Oh I'm fed up with all this suspense. Are you going through or not?
Kaliban No. It's a trap.

Widow Duffcake goes round behind Kaliban

Widow Duffcake *(to audience)* If you want something done, do it yourself.
Omar, Widow Duffcake and **Marco** *(together)* NOW!
Audience and **all on stage** SAUCEPANS.

Widow Duffcake pushes Kaliban through the machine, a loud hooter sounds, he turns and falls, Prince, Sinbad etc., catch him. They prop him up on a chair

Prince Look at that!
Raisin It's curtains for him!
Kashoo Sleeping like a baby.
Sinbad We've done it!
Everyone on stage HOORAY!
Sinbad Fetch Genius.

Omar and Marco go off and bring on Genius

Genius Did it work?
Prince Did it work? Look.
Raisin You're a genius, Genius.
Prince *(removing the lamp from Kaliban's head, as he sleeps)* Genius. I think this is yours.
Genius *(taking the lamp)* Thank you. I'm free at last.

Song No 14

A song sung by all on stage, "Raindrops Keep falling on (his) Head", or "Born Free" or "It's a Hap, Hap, Happy day" or another. They group around the sleeping Kaliban and sing to him

If the former is chosen, the following words are suggested:

All   Raindrops keep falling on his head.
          Kaliban's eyes have just been too big for his head,
          Nothing seems to fit.
          Those raindrops keep falling on his head, they keep falling,
          But there's one thing we know,
          The blues he sent to greet us, won't defeat us,
          It won't be long til happiness comes round to greet us
Genius   And now I'm free, nothing's worrying me.
All   So we did some talking to this one,
          And we said we didn't like the way he got things done
          SLEEPING ON THE JOB
          So, raindrops keep falling on his head, they keep falling,
          But there's one thing we know,
          The blues he sent to greet us, won't defeat us.
          It won't be long til happiness comes round to meet us
          Because I'm free, nothing's worrying me.

At the end of the song

Prince Back home everybody.
Sinbad And return the stone to its rightful owner.
Prince *(to Raisin)* And a wedding I hope?
Raisin You just try to escape.
Kashoo I think you mean two weddings.
Widow Duffcake So it's curtains for Sinbad too.

They all exit, waving to the audience

Curtain

Scene 4

*On the way home. This interact scene, to allow finale costume changes and
scene setting, may be played in front of tabs, or a frontcloth showing a desert
scene, an oasis, or whatever*

Enter Marco and Omar. They have brooms and start sweeping up the stage

Marco Have you put the cat out?
Omar I didn't even know it was on fire.
Marco That's it then.
Omar Until tomorrow.
Marco *(seeing the audience)* Oh, look, they're still here.
Omar I thought they'd gone home.
Marco Shall we tell them?
Omar Yes, tell them.

Marco You've been the best audience we've had - tonight.

Omar I know. They want to sing a song. We nearly forgot. We always sing a song now, don't we?

Marco Which song shall we sing then?

Omar What about that Sheikh of Araby song?

Marco Yes, that was a good one. Let's sing that.

Enter Sultan and Shererazade, already changed for the finale

Sultan Just a minute. That's my song.

Omar We'd better let him help.

Schererazade Or it might be curtains for you.

Sultan I should think so.

Schererazade You take that half, and we'll take this half.

Marco Right.

Omar Our half can sing better etc.,

Marco and Omar bring on the words, or they are lowered down

Song 15

Community number. A verse from "The Sheikh of Araby" or another. The usual additions of a competition, prize winners, birthday gifts etc., can all be included here

At the end of the song, all exit

To a fanfare the curtains open

Scene 5

The interior of Sultan Shahriar's palace. This can be as for Act 1 Scene 2 or may be a new set, the Grand Entrance, or Reception Hall

The cast enter in order, and take their bows as the finale song is sung

Song No 16

"On a Wonderful Day Like Today" or any up-tempo number from the show

The guests are arriving for the wedding of The Kalandar Prince to Princess Raisin

Suggested walk-down order

Junior chorus, dragons etc.,
Senior Chorus
Eric and Dragon

Mesrour
Ali Baba and Genius
Omar and Marco
Kaliban and Widow Duffcake
Sinbad and Kashoo
Sultan and Schererazade

Now, to a cheer, enter Prince Ahmed and Princess Raisin, who take their bows

Schererazade *(stepping forward)*
The tale is told, our story ends.
It's time to say good-bye, dear friends.
And wish you all again, once more,
The best a New Year has in store,
We hope our panto brought you cheer,
And hope to see you all next year.

The final verse is sung as the cast wave good-bye

Final curtain

FURNITURE AND PROPERTY LIST

ACT 1

Scene 1

Off stage: Giant hammer for **Widow Duffcake**
Personal: **Omar**, hand-held recording machine
Marco, rubber mallet
Kaliban, lamp (carried throughout) spare wallet
Prince's servant, large stone on cushion
Mesrour, scimitar (carried throughout)

Scene 2

On stage: Two seats, or cushions
Personal: **Kaliban**, false jewel
Slave, stone on cushion
Maidens, ostrich fans
Mesrour, TV Times
Sultan, handkerchief
Widow Duffcake, large saucepan and ladle

Scene 4

On stage: Various markets stalls with stock, including a pottery stall, and carpet marked "Magic Carpet"
Off Stage: "Shoutometer" for **Genius**
Personal: **Omar**, papers
Kaliban, magic stone

Scene 6

On stage: Chairs or cushions, as before
Off stage: "Enlivening Machine" for **Genius** (see Production Notes)
Personal: **Omar**, Teddy Bear

ACT 2

Scene 1

On stage: Various debris; bones, hanging spiders, cobwebs, "Keep Out" notice etc., Seat large enough for three
Personal: **Kashoo**, handkerchief for bandage
Mini-dragon, magic stone
Widow Duffcake, umbrella or rolling-pin
Omar and **Marco**, various weapons and armour

Scene 2

Personal:	**Widow Duffcake**, baseball bat or large rolling-pin (for next scene also)

Scene 3

On stage:	Table and two chairs, large bottle of "Camel Oil", two glasses, television cut-out
Off stage:	"Enlivening Machine" for **Genius**
Personal:	**Genius**, jug of beer
	Ali Baba, Kaliban and **Genius**, scimitars
	Raisin, magic stone

Scene 4

Off stage:	Community song words
Personal:	**Omar** and **Marco**, brooms

LIGHTING PLOT

ACT 1

Scene 1

Open:	Bright exterior lighting	Page 1
Cue 1:	As **Kaliban** enters	Page 2
	Green spot on wings, cut as he walks on stage	
Cue 2:	As **Widow Duffcake** goes down into audience	Page 9
	Houselights up, fade as she goes back on stage	
Cue 3:	As **Widow Duffcake** exits	Page 12
	Blackout	

Scene 2

Open:	Bright interior lighting	Page 12
Cue 4:	As **Genius** enters	Page 13
	Flash. Lights up and down quickly	
Cue 5:	As curtains close	Page 18
	Blackout	

Scene 3

Open:	Bright exterior lighting	Page 18

Cue 6: As **Genius** waves arms   Page 19
Lights up and down as curtains open

Scene 4

Open: Bright exterior lighting   Page 19

Cue 7: **Widow Duffcake**, "Can't find his Weetabix" Page 23
Lights dim. Lightning flashes
Cue 8: **Widow Duffcake**, "Turning into cucumber"   Page 24
Lightning flashes up to maximum
Cue 9: **Widow Duffcake**, "I want me mum"   Page 24
Lightning flashes fade out. Normal lighting up

Scene 5

Open: Bright exterior lighting   Page 26

Scene 6

Open: Bright interior lighting   Page 28

Cue 10: As **Kashoo** and **Genius** stand on carpet Page 32
Spot on carpet. All other lights fade out
Cue 11: **Sinbad**, "Take us to dragon's cave"   Page 32
Lights flash
Cue 12: **Sinbad**, "It really works"   Page 32
Slowly fade spot

ACT 2

Scene 1

Open: Dim interior lighting   Page 33

Cue 13: As **Kashoo** and **Sinbad** enter   Page 33
Slowly bring up lighting
Cue 14: As **Dragon** roars (off)   Page 36
Shadow of Dragon's head on back curtain
Cue 15: **Kashoo**, "Is that your daddy?"   Page 37
Shadow of Dragon's head on back curtain again
Cue 16: As **Dragon** enters   Page 37
Flashing lights
Cue 17: As curtain closes   Page 40
Slowly fade lights

Scene 2

Scene 3

Scene 4

Scene 5

EFFECTS PLOT

General suggestions are given below. The amount, and diversity of effects will depend upon what the director has at his disposal. For instance, a "crash" may be cymbals crashing, a drum roll, or simply chords on the piano etc., The use of appropriate effect sounds can bring a pantomime to life, and their value should not be underestimated.

The effects for the cave scene (Act 2 Sc 1) are the most complex here. The "dragon roars" will probably need to be pre-recorded. The echoes may also be pre-recorded, or could be shouted through a megaphone from backstage. You may wish to experiment to obtain the best effect for your theatre here.

You may wish to have "entry music" for some of your characters. This can take the form of a properly orchestrated piece, or simply a couple of chords on the piano.

ACT 1

PRODUCTION NOTES

Scenery. Most of the scenery in this pantomime is fairly straightforward. A strongly eastern, exotic atmosphere is needed here. There is a wonderful opportunity to allow your sense of colour full reign, both with scenery and costumes. The cave scene should, in contrast, be mysterious, cluttered and subdued, with the colourful dragons brightening it all up. All the interact scenes can be performed in front of a frontcloth, if these are to be used, or may be played in front of tabs.

Costumes. As I have said above, the costumes should be as colourful and elaborate as you can manage. **Kaliban** is a sort of Abanazar figure, and can have something of a magician about him. **Genius** a typical Genie of the Lamp. The **Sultan** is a rather colourful and overdressed exotic ruler, with the ladies, **Schererazade, Raisin, Kashoo** and the ladies of the palace chorus, wearing the traditional harem-trouser and waistcoat costumes in many colours. Curled shoes and elaborate headwear, turbans, decorated, or ostrich, fans for the slave-girls etc., will all add greatly to the effect.

Kaliban, Sultan, Schererazade, Raisin, Ahmed, Mesrour, Sinbad, Kashoo, Omar, Marco, Ali Baba, Genius and **Eric** can all wear one costume throughout, if desired, with the possibility of changes for the finale. The exception is, of course, **Widow Duffcake**, where provision (and time) has been allowed for several costume changes to be made. You might want to change **Omar** and **Marco** for the scene where they go through the machine, and also got up in some form of armour for their entry to the cave. **Kaliban** also, can be changed into heavy bandages for the scene where he goes through the machine. **Kaliban** and **Ali Baba** can be more richly costumed when they become (temporarily) rich, but this is not essential. **Eric** can be dressed as a ghost, a skeleton, a knome or goblin, or whatever. The **Mini-dragons** should in some way reflect the main dragon's costume. The **Dragon** should be an elaborate affair, inspired by Chinese dragon designs. He can be one, large man, a "panto horse" pair, or a chain, as for the traditional Chinese dragon.

Property. The "Enlivening Machine" can be a very simple affair. Two separate pieces of wood, each on its own stand, and painted metallic, or very colourful, can be brought on and stood parallel to each other (possibly with an extra piece that can be added to the top on stage) with room to walk between. Alternatively, this could be a sort of door-frame affair, like an airport security screen, again, painted as suggested.

A "Shoutometer" may be used in Act 1 Sc 4. This will be a giant, painted, mock thermometer, with moveable "mercury" that is operated by Genius from the back.

You will need some scimitars, or possibly spears for **Mesrour**, and the guards etc., Also a "Keep out" notice for the cave scene. All other properties are easily obtained items in general use.

I wish you, and your audience, great fun with this pantomime.

Jim Sperinck